"Petra Carlsson Redell is unique among radical theologians. Instead of talking about creativity and imagination, she does theology that is actually creative and imaginative. Moreover, her theological discourse addresses the visual arts, also extremely rare among radical theologians. But Carlsson Redell goes even further, her work not only addresses the visual arts, but is formed by and through her engagement Russian Constructivism—one of the more radical aesthetic and political practices of the early twentieth-century avant-garde—and the paintings and writings of Liubov Popova (1889–1924) in particular. Carlsson Redell does theology, *performs* and *improvises* a theology that resembles Popova's paintings and writings, shapes of powerful color that form a loosely yet taught assemblage composed of elements—an actual, material "thing" that works in the world—that contributes to its complexity and mystery, and in the process, perhaps even changes it."

—Daniel A. Siedell, Ph.D. art historian, educator,
and curator, New York City

"Petra Carlsson Redell's new book is an illustration of what can happen when new voices and fresh perspectives are introduced into established traditions of thought. By inserting Liubov Popova, one of the most important women artists of the Russian avant-garde, into the tradition of radical theology, Carlsson Redell reframes theological ideas in ways which allow her to engage directly with current political and ecological issues. Popova helps the author rethink the spiritual dimension of matter and to address the environmental crisis, a problem which, as far as it hinges on human existence, is ultimately theological in nature. The book is both an original contribution to the field of theology through the arts and to a radical theology, which confronts boldly problems of modernity."

—Clemena Antonova, author of Visual Thought in Russian Religious
Philosophy *(Routledge, 2020), and Research Director of the Eurasia in*
Global Dialogue Programme, Institute for Human Sciences, Vienna

Avantgarde Art and Radical Material Theology

In conversation with twentieth-century materialist art and thought, this book presents a radical theology that engages directly with the political and ecological issues of our time.

The book introduces a new thinker to the theological sphere, Russian avantgarde artist Liubov Popova (1889–1924). She was a woman acknowledged for her artistic and intellectual talent and yet is never discussed in relation to the twentieth-century thinkers with whom her ideas have obvious connections. Popova's art and thought are discussed together with thinkers like Walter Benjamin, Donna Haraway, Gilles Deleuze and Paul Tillich, along with ecotheological and theopolitical perspectives. Inspired by the activist creativity of avantgarde art, the book's final chapter, playfully yet with deadly seriousness, presents a manifesto for radical theology today.

This is a work of theological activism that demonstrates the benefit of allowing new voices into the conversations around art, spirituality and our planet. As such, it will be of keen interest to academics in Theology, Religion and the Arts and the Philosophy of Religion.

Petra Carlsson Redell is an Associate Professor of Systematic Theology at Stockholm School of Theology, Sweden. She has published multiple times on religion, philosophy and art in journals such as *Studia Theologica* and *The Oxford Journal of Literature & Theology*, and in books including *Mysticism as Revolt* (2014) and *Foucault, Art, and Radical Theology* (2018).

Routledge Focus on Religion

Amoris Laetitia and the Spirit of Vatican II
The Source of Controversy
Mariusz Biliniewicz

Muslim and Jew
Origins, Growth, Resentment
Aaron W Hughes

The Bible and Digital Millennials
David G. Ford, Joshua L. Mann and Peter M. Phillips

The Fourth Secularisation
Autonomy of Individual Lifestyles
Luigi Berzano

Narratives of Faith from the Haiti Earthquake
Religion, Natural Hazards and Disaster Response
Roger P. Abbott and Robert S. White

The Bible, Social Media and Digital Culture
Peter M. Phillips

Religious Studies and the Goal of Interdisciplinarity
Brent Smith

Visual Thought in Russian Religious Philosophy
Pavel Florensky's Theory of the Icon
Clemena Antonova

American Babylon
Christianity and Democracy Before and After Trump
Philip S. Gorski

Avantgarde Art and Radical Material Theology
A Manifesto
Petra Carlsson Redell

For more information about this series, please visit:
https://www.routledge.com/Routledge-Focus-on-Religion/book-series/RFR

Avantgarde Art and Radical Material Theology
A Manifesto

Petra Carlsson Redell

LONDON AND NEW YORK

First published 2021
by Routledge
2 Park Square, Milton Park, Abingdon, Oxon OX14 4RN

and by Routledge
52 Vanderbilt Avenue, New York, NY 10017

Routledge is an imprint of the Taylor & Francis Group, an informa
business

British Library Cataloguing-in-Publication Data
A catalogue record for this book is available from the British Library

Library of Congress Cataloging-in-Publication Data
A catalog record has been requested for this book

ISBN: 978-0-367-18871-9 (hbk)

ISBN: 978-0-4291-9893-9 (ebk)

Typeset in Times New Roman
by Deanta Global Publishing Services, Chennai, India

Contents

Foreword

Jeffrey W. Robbins

A manifesto is a literary form of concentrated theoretical energy intended to activate a change in the basic orientation to thought and action. It is distinct from the essay that is meant to be an analytic, speculative or interpretative proposal. The manifesto is distinct in that it is a public declaration, a staking of ground, a call to action. As Petra Carlsson Redell eloquently states at the very outset of this book, manifestos

> add truths to the multiplicity of reality. They make public what is already there but mute. Manifestos hand a megaphone to the murmur, not in order to have the last say—the totality of manifestos is always plural—but to raise muted voices.

In this way, the manifesto is the preferred mode of communication for a radical theology.

Likewise, with regard to the avantgarde, it is marked by its daring and unorthodox experimentation. While it might play fast and loose with tradition, at the same time it is driven by a seriousness of purpose to create anew, to make alternative assemblages, to associate the formerly disassociated, disregarded, neglected and obscured. It too by its very nature is befitting a radical theology.

Finally, consider the idea of materiality, not only the stuff of earth, nature and science, of physical laws, of genetics and of economic determinism, but the materiality of art, ritual and technology, of the task of construction, of the fetishised object, of commodities and machines. We know, of course, the myriad of ways by which the material has been denigrated. We know—or at least we are coming to appreciate—the consequences that this ideational privileging of mind over matter and spirit over flesh has when it comes to our present ecological crisis. So, if to be radical means at least partly to get at the roots of the thing in question, a radical theology must be by definition a material theology.

All of which begs the question: what is radical theology? It has been defined as a post-liberal tradition of thought that emerges out of the death of God movement of the 1960s. It is neither theistic nor atheistic, but still recognises God as a formulation of extremity that gets at the root of thought and opens up pathways for a thinking that knows no bounds. In this way, the idea of God and the desire for God outlive the death of God, and thus, while emerging out of the death of God movement radical theology is no longer bound by it.[1]

While the tradition of radical theology has enjoyed something of a revival first beginning with its reinvigoration by the link established with deconstruction and postmodernism through such figures as Mark C. Taylor, Carl Raschke, Charles E. Winquist and Edith Wyschogrod and more recently by its turn to the political and the material, its provenance has remained a limited one.[2] It has largely been the expression of a white, male, Euro-American perspective. It has failed to pursue the obvious connections between itself and other movements in contemporary religious life and theological thought such as liberationist, process, feminist, queer and/or critical race theory. It is not that radical theology has been openly hostile to any of these movements; rather, it is a question of radical theology's casual disregard, or perhaps better, structural blindness.

Charles Mills' *Racial Contract* provides the classic template for how white privilege functions in an unacknowledged way in modern Western philosophy and moral theory.[3] No matter the height of our lofty moral ideals—or maybe the price for them—there is a casual and consistent, but still shocking, insensitivity to racial subjugation. The social contract is built on dehumanisation. The social contract is a racial contract insofar as structural discrimination is the norm. The moral autonomy, independence and responsibility exalted within modern liberalism was reserved only for the few. Mills' point, of course, is that this reality should not be shocking at all for those who take account of race, power and domination in their moral calculations. In other words, it is only a shock to those who have bought into the fiction of the universal man who is presumed to be the fount of right and responsible thought and action.

Likewise, from the Black Liberationist theologian James H. Cone, throughout his career he took inspiration and guidance from, and wrestled with, the legacy of the modern, white, European, Protestant theological tradition. While early on he was drawn to the power and clarity of Karl Barth's neo-orthodoxy, he eventually gravitated more to those who gave credence to the ambiguities of human experience, most especially Paul Tillich and Reinhold Niebuhr. It was the appreciation of the tragic nature of history and the structural nature of sin, in particular, that drew Cone to Niebuhr. But in Cone's final book, *The Cross and the Lynching Tree*, Niebuhr was seen in a different light.[4] For by his theological methodology and distinctive insights, he more than others should have been attuned to the suffering of African Americans and the sinfulness, pride and obliviousness of white American Christians. He more than others should have appreciated the tragic irony associated with Jesus' death as an innocent victim and the thousands of those lynched at the hands of white mobs in defence of certain notions of nation and faith. Cones' point, like Mills', is that these lynchings were not an accident, aberration or failure of the Christian imagination, but rather an expression of its full lethality. Niebuhr's obliviousness or indifference, therefore, was in no way exemplary, but all too tragically common.

With respect to Paul Tillich, much has been made of his centrality to the patrilineage of radical theology.[5] His analysis of the dynamics of faith embraced—even defined faith in terms of—existential doubt. Faith was portrayed as the courage to pass through the crucible of the death of God. Further, his theology of culture situated the work of the theologian outside the safe confines of the church wherein the worlds of modern art, literature, consumerist society, ethno-nationalism and other world religions raised questions of ultimacy. But it is precisely at this point where this book is at its most disruptive. For while Tillich's method of correlation seeks to situate the sacred within the profane and blur the boundaries between faith and doubt, Petra Carlsson Redell shows how Tillich nevertheless keeps certain boundaries intact. Specifically, the distinctions between high art and low art, between the original and the copy, the creative and the constructive, and thus by extension Tillich unwittingly maintains the fundamental distinction between the spiritual and the material.

Make no mistake, this book is not intended as a detailed critical study or exposition of Tillich. Indeed, Carlsson Redell makes clear that she is more interested in "adding ways of thinking than about critiquing existing ways". But it is nevertheless by this critique that the author not only opens herself to the avantgarde of Russian constructivist art, but also in so doing upends the patrilineage of radical theology where we, in her words, finally "arrive at an experimental, playful yet serious manifesto for radical theology—a manifesto for second theology constructors of our time". It is a new theology, to be sure, but "not for the sake of theology itself—not to rescue a threatened theological language from extinction due to lack of meaning—but for the sake of the planet".

What I find most thrilling and promising in this book—indeed, in Carlsson Redell's unfolding theological project more generally—is not only its bold ambition (e.g., "follow my reasoning through these pages and you will be given my suggestion of how theology may help save the planet"), but its always experimental and heterodoxical path for getting there. Where else—or in what other author—does one find a direct path from Lynn White

Jr.'s ground-breaking article on "The Historical Roots of Our Ecological Crisis", to the cyborg, the fetishised object and the celestial machine? Where ecotheologies abound in the reanimation of spirit in nature, Carlsson Redell runs full speed ahead to the world of reproduction and technology. Drawing from Walter Benjamin's distinction between first and second technology, the author's embrace of the technological should not be taken as a quest for mastery or control, but an affirmation of relationality in which "humanity and nature are not seen as entities, as objects for technology, but technology is understood more like a verb at work in the very relationality that makes humanity and nature appear". This is not a return to a lost Eden but a recognition of the contingency of all things and the fragility of the world of our very own making. Clear-eyed and sober, yet also abundantly playful. In this book we encounter a world of devastation, extinction and domination, but also of kitsch and super-abundance, and a way of thinking unmoored from any origin, from any longing for an Eden that never was.

Consider, for instance, the details for what is at stake in the conceptual move from the face to the machine that Carlsson Redell suggests. If, as she maintains, "the image of Jesus' face has remained largely the same from the sixth century until the present day", it must also be pointed out that the face has been central to ethical considerations of moral responsibility, especially for those following the lead of Emmanuel Levinas. It is thought that the face-to-face encounter presents an absolute moral demand on the self for the other and that the face transcends ordinary moral deliberations and categories. It is in this context that one must appreciate how the move from the face to the machine not only entails a critique of representation but a willing and deliberate distortion and transformation of centuries of Christian iconography and piety. Whether it is the face, the nose, the heart, the body, the mind or the spirit, they are all elements of reality that take part in the ongoing construction of the world. Just as no single element can be singled out from a constructivist perspective, so too is the image of Jesus fair game. There are no exceptions.

As Carlsson Redell repeatedly makes clear, it is not about replacing but adding, not about deleting but complementing, and thereby opening up and activating new and different possibilities. This includes now thinking of Christ less in terms of classical trinitarian debates over substance and identity and more in terms of event and action. And because there are no exceptions, the Christ event is not a once and for all singular event—at least no more so or no less so than any and all events are singularities—but in her words "is what it does—constantly moving, stuck in its repetitious motion, persistently repeating its motion of sinking/rising, dying/resurrecting through theological analysis, in art as well as collective and individual experiences of faith".

The resonances on this point with the previously cited work from Cone are profound. Carlsson Redell implores us not to confine the Christ event to ancient history but to note its persistent repetition. Likewise, Cone points to the structural similarities between the cross and the lynching tree where both are "symbols of terror, instruments of torture and execution, reserved primarily for slaves, criminals and insurrectionists".[6] By this structural similarity, we might realise that Jesus' death was not an isolated incident. On the contrary, what both the cross and the lynching tree reveal is not a single, exclusive point in human history wherein an innocent victim was made to die, but that this is a terrible truth that societies repeat, almost ineluctably.

What gives this work its manifesto quality is its radically inclusive spirit. It is critical, to be sure, but even more, it is a work of construction inspired by the avantgarde constructivists who dared to build a better world. Carlsson Redell gives us a theology in which everything is at stake and nothing is safe. In so doing, she redirects Christian thought away from the task of salvation or rehabilitation. She also, in a graceful but still deliberate fashion, redirects the tradition of radical theology away from its traditional historical archive. Hers is a not a theology in crisis, but a theology for a world in crisis. As such, it is exactly what we need here and now.

Notes

1 See Jeffrey W. Robbins, *Radical Theology: A Vision for Change* (Bloomington: Indiana University Press, 2016).
2 For an excellent survey of this revival and reinvigoration, see Jordan E. Miller, *Resisting Theology, Furious Hope: Secular Political Theology and Social Movements* (New York: Palgrave Macmillan, 2019).
3 Charles Mills, *The Racial Contract* (Ithaca: Cornell University Press, 1999).
4 James H. Cone, *The Cross and the Lynching Tree* (New York: Orbis, 2013).
5 See especially Russell Re Manning, ed., *Retrieving the Radical Tillich: His Legacy and Contemporary Importance* (New York: Palgrave Macmillan, 2015).
6 Cone, *The Cross and the Lynching Tree*, 31.

Preface

This book is an attempt to advance the approach advocated by Lynn White Jr. in his widely influential article published more than fifty years ago: that is, to address the current environmental crisis not by inventing a new religion or embracing some new-old animist faith in the spirits inhabiting nature, but by critically and creatively reconsidering "our old one". Here I offer my proposal as to how a re-envisioned Christian theology may help save the planet. I realise the goal is overly ambitious, but there is no time for shyness or conceit. This is what I have come up with at this stage—no more, no less. It cannot be proffered as *the* sole solution, certainly, but as one contribution among many emerging that may assist a positive development. This approach has changed my way of thinking and living, and it could do something similar for you. Either way, you can help us all think further, whether in this direction or another.

The chapters to come explore our old Christian religion—broadly understood as a set of ideas that infuse our political reality in the material world, as well as our concrete everyday lives—by way of twentieth-century thinkers including Walter Benjamin, Donna Haraway and Gilles Deleuze, entered primarily through the Russian constructivist artist and thinker Liubov Popova (1889–1924). Through Popova we encounter a way of understanding theology that affects how we view technology, things, matter in general, time and space, as well as our possibilities to act. Matter stands forth as *spiritual* because matter and construction surpasses the limits of our imagination. This book introduces a theology grounded in matter: a radical material theology in which the spiritual is material, and the material is political and enigmatic. Inspired by the avantgarde artists, by orthodox iconography and liturgy and by the thinkers and activists discussed, we explore a range of interrelated notions in five chapters: (1) the backdrop, which develops themes in theology and art that are deployed in later chapters; (2) the theologian as cyborg and as constructor; (3) a *second theology* modelled on Walter Benjamin's *second technology*, one not focused on Christian truth as such but on the relationship between humanity and the ideas of Christian truth; (4) Christ as machine and (5) an eschatology out of joint. Finally, we arrive at an experimental and playful yet serious manifesto for radical material theology—a manifesto for second-theology constructors of our time.

After the First World War, the popular theologian Paul Tillich was likewise convinced that a new Protestant theology was needed. The error of late nineteenth-century theology, he argued, was that religion had become separated from culture. Religion had lost contact with culture and theological language had become meaningless, which is why Tillich pointed towards the correlation between the two. Beneath all questions regarding human life, he contended, is the primordial question: "What does it mean to exist?" "Existence is the question which underlies all other questions" and God, understood as the ground of being, holds the answer. God beyond God, God beyond theism—God constitutes meaning. "Existence", Tillich wrote, "is the fundamental problem which precedes all specific problems concerning man".[1] Today, once again, we find ourselves in a situation crying out for new theology—not for the sake of theology per se, not to rescue a threatened theological language from extinction due to lack of meaning, but for the sake of the planet.

The critical question of our time does relate to existence, but less to its meaning than to its perseverance. Existence is threatened, which is why a new theology is needed not to ponder the "meaning" of life but to suggest ways of living, thinking and believing that will enable continued human existence in humble respect for the multiplicity of life. We need theologies that act: we need act-thinking, think-acting theologies that encourage construction and reconstruction of our world, politically and ecologically.[2] "Expediency!" Popova would say. Function and construction should lead the way towards what actually creates the world anew. Not solely according to our own will, however, but according to the will of every element of reality.[3] By bringing together the key points of the preceding chapters, the manifesto for second theology presented in the conclusion wants to contribute to such a theological development. As shall become evident, however, the expediency evolving through the pages of this book is—albeit pragmatic—far from any plain pragmatism.

Thus, the book also contributes to the experimental and dispersed thought tradition reaching back to the death of God-theology movement of the 1960s, which in turn would not have appeared without the ground having been prepared by Tillich. The encounter with Thomas J. J. Altizer (1927–2018) and his immanent metaphysics was an important starting point for me—I started using the concept of *radical theology* to describe my own work, inspired by his choice of the term over *death-of-God* theology. To label radical theology a "thought tradition" or a "school of theology" seems unfitting, however, since every expression using the term goes its own way. Thinkers like Jeffrey W. Robbins, Clayton Crockett, Katharine Sarah Moody, Ward Blanton, Noëlle Vahanian, Lissa McCullough, Christopher Rodkey, Peter Rollins, Ulf Dalferth and Carl Raschke, to name a few, all describe their contributions as radical theology but are working only roughly in the same direction. Bo Sanders at *Homebrewed Christianity* suggests a definition:

> A theological approach that is not tied to a congregation, denomination or other sanctioning body. The freedom of not being anchored in a confessional approach allows thinkers to interact with daring, innovative and contemporary schools of thought without consequence of consideration of how the outcome will impact faith communities (at least not primarily).[4]

Katharine Sarah Moody's discussion on the presence of radical theology in communities of emergent Christianity complicates the definition immediately, though.[5] Moody's work shows that radical theology may very well inspire, and even emerge from, actual church communities and congregations. To me, radical theology is about playfulness and serious disrespect, about rearranging and reconstructing theology for the sake of God and humanity, for the sake of the multiplicity of life—whether within, at the fringes of, or outside Christian communities and church life. I invoke "serious disrespect" because I suspect that experimental or even blasphemous treatments of the theological heritage may keep us from creating eternal monuments that lead to lifelessness, oppression and destruction. Disobedient playfulness, in humble respect for the mystery of things, for the inherited wisdom of traditions, yet adding thoughts, words, actions, objects to the surface of appearances, may construct the world anew. While aiming to reconsider key theological aspects, I am not claiming that the ideas presented are entirely new. Rather, ideas inherited from the theological past are experimentally combined in new constellations in order to permit new aspects to stand forth.

While the book develops the "material radical theology with a political edge" of my previous work, it also further explores a path travelled by many others, and I want to mention a few. I cite them in part to situate the current contribution, hence, to facilitate the reading, but more importantly to underline the collectivity of thinking. As theology constructors, we are mechanics using bits and pieces manufactured by others, then leaving our constructions to further reconstruction or deconstruction. Hence, like Blanton, Crockett, Robbins and Vahanian, I aim to direct religious and spiritual energies into political, this-worldly transformation, while also showing that material and spiritual ideas and practices are in no way opposed.[6] In their *Insurrectionist Manifesto*, the four authors play with the manifesto format and even write four new gospels. This is not out of hubris, but is a way of staying true to the creativity of early Christianity—in keeping with the first gospel writers who, of course, were many more than four, as a multitude of gospels were circulating before four were finally chosen as canonical.[7] If the radical theology of the 1960s—with the 1965 "Is God Dead?" cover of *Time* magazine as its iconic symbol—dealt primarily with issues of Christian truth and meaningfulness, radical theology today should pave the way for a new political theology, they argue, one that chooses another path than that of Carl Schmitt and his theopolitical logics of the One.[8] Not because contemporary political theology can be equated with the Schmittian thought structure but because the political aspect of radical theology's trajectory is still under development and political theology is in need of more voices.[9] Hence I accept Blanton, Crockett, Robbins and Vahanian's invitation to "anyone and everyone" to "participate in the production of new forms of news worthy of the name 'good'"—and I hereby also pass it on to you.[10]

The current book also has what I like to think of as big cousins in books like Laurel C. Schneider's *Beyond Monotheism* (2007) and Catherine Keller's *Political Theology of the Earth* (2018), to name two. It relates to and is inspired by the post-Christian experimental theology by Mattias Martinson, the theological activism explored by Ulrich Schmiedel, the Hegelian political theology of Tommie Lynch, the Scandinavian Creation Theology movement, the exegetical critique of Christian populism by Hanna Strømmen, the spiritual activism of knitting described by Anna Fisk, Susanne Wigorts Yngvesson's technotheology, the messianic prophetism discussed by Jayne Svenungsson, the political theology of Judaism described by Alana Vincent, Kamilla Skarström Hinojosa's analyses of the performative Qumran theology, the patient Derridean theological resistance introduced by Agata Bielik-Robson, the radically inclusive pastoral theology of Mark Godin, the force of vulnerability explored by Joseph Sverker, the this-life-visionary of Martin Hägglund, the architectural entanglements of David Capener, the catacombic theology of Josef Gustafsson, the growing LGBTQ+ theology movement, the climate actions and refugee volunteer work in every congregation I visit, the wisdom of pastors, priests and everyday believers, and by pastors like Lena Bergström who are using their entire evangelisation worktime to make sure the young are safe at the #FridaysForFuture climate demonstrations—and by many more, of course.

To me, radical theology is an open field for theological experimentation, within or outside church life, a field for a theology that is prepared to lose itself over and over again, in transformation, on trial, for a world in which the multiplicity of life expresses itself to infinity.

Notes

1 Paul Tillich, *Systematic Theology I* (Chicago: University of Chicago Press, 1951), 1:65.
2 The notion of "think-acting" is inspired by Lissa McCullough, "D. G. Leahy", in *Palgrave Handbook of Radical Theology*, eds. Christopher D. Rodkey and Jordan E. Miller (New York: Palgrave Macmillan, 2019), 279.
3 Liubov Popova, "On a Precise Criterion, on Ballet Steps, on Deck Equipment for Warships, on Picasso's Latest Portraits, and on the Observation Tower at the Military Camouflage School at Kuntsevo (a Few Thoughts that Came to Mind During the Vocal and Ballet Numbers at the Krivoi Dzhimmi Summer Theater in Moscow in the Summer of 1922)", in *Liubov Popova*, eds. Dimitri V. Sarabianov and Natalia L. Adaskina, trans. Marian Schwartz (New York: Harry N. Abrams, 1990), 380–381.
4 Bo Sanders, "Radical Theology Cliff Notes", *Homebrewed Christianity*, https://homebrewedchristianity.com/2013/07/23/radical-theology-cliff-notes/.
5 Katharine Sarah Moody, *Radical Theology and Emerging Christianity: Deconstruction, Materialism and Religious Practices* (Dorchester: Ashgate, 2015).
6 Ward Blanton, Clayton Crockett, Jeffrey W. Robbins, and Noëlle Vahanian, "Introduction: What is Insurrectionist Theology?", in *An Insurrectionist Manifesto: Four New Gospels for a Radical Politics*, eds. Ward Blanton, Clayton Crockett, Jeffrey W. Robbins, and Noëlle Vahanian (New York: Columbia University Press, 2016), 13.
7 Blanton et al., "Introduction: What is Insurrectionist Theology?", 17.
8 Blanton et al., "Introduction: What is Insurrectionist Theology?", 2.
9 Graham Ward has sketched the contours of a contemporary political theology beyond the Schmittian conception of theology in several articles and books like *Christ and Culture* (Chichester: Wiley Blackwell, 2015) and *The Politics of Discipleship: Becoming Postmaterial Citizens* (Grand Rapids: Baker, 2009). His political theology is discussed and developed by Peter Carlsson in *Teologi som Kritik: Graham Ward och den postsekulära hermeneutiken* (Göteborg: Göteborgs universitet, 2017). Also in Scandinavia, the political theology of the Lutheran tradition has been explored by thinkers such as Elisabeth Gerle, Carl-Henrik Grenholm, Göran Gunner and others; see, for example, Carl-Henrik Grenholm and Göran Gunner, eds., *Lutheran Identity and Political Theology* (Cambridge: Clarke, 2015). The field of liturgical theology expresses an understanding of the political aspects of theology in terms of concrete Christian life with thinkers like Cláudio Carvalhaes; political theology in the Pentecostal tradition is explored by Amos Young; and the potential references continue.
10 Blanton et al., "Introduction: What is Insurrectionist Theology?", 18.

Introduction
Radical material theology and the Earth

Writing in the borderland between theology and art means dealing with a deeply rooted dichotomy between the material and the spiritual. To many in Western Christian parts of the world the very idea that a created, material composition could contain spiritual *reality*—not merely spiritual *meaning*—is contradictory. In fact, the idea of an object of any kind as itself a spiritual reality is odd to many Christian or post-Christian cultures. As the historian of technology Lynn White Jr. wrote in his groundbreaking article of 1967: "To a Christian a tree can be no more than a physical fact".[1] White famously argued in this controversial article that the inherited, often unconscious Christian worldview according to which nature is placed under the *dominion* of man is a key to understanding the disastrous development of our environmental history. He suggested that the very notion of a "sacred tree" is outlandish to the very ethos of the West because Christian missionaries have been chopping down sacred trees for two millennia. They have done so precisely because, from a Christian viewpoint, the assumption of a spiritual reality in nature is idolatrous.

White argued that we must clarify our thinking in relation to the ecological crisis by looking at the presuppositions that underlie Western technology and science—the God-man-nature relationship being one of those presuppositions. In his words, "more science and more technology are not going to get us out of the present ecological crisis until we find a new religion, or rethink our old one".[2] Only when religion is rethought, he reasoned, may science and technology be employed to assist the preservation of the Earth. Over the intervening five decades, White's article has been criticised for its sweeping interpretation of Christianity even while his overall ambition has been developed by many.[3] Nevertheless, apart from the possibility of getting us "out of" the ecological crisis rather than handling or mitigating its consequences, his reasoning is still pertinent and applicable today.[4] Indeed, this harbinger article serves as a reminder of the long-term collective negligence of the accelerating degradation of the Earth's ecosystems. White strikes a balance between trusting technology to mitigate the environmental crisis versus seeing technology as its cause—a balanced view of technology that we shall encounter in a different form in Russian avantgarde art and thought in the pages to come.

Material sacrality

Many have rethought the Western ideas that lie beneath the destruction of the planet since White's article was first published. A growing awareness of the need to find new presuppositional bridges between humanity and nature is expressed directly or indirectly in the practical turn emerging in several theoretical fields: for example, in the recent hype of new materialism; in the broad theoretical interest in materiality and space, not to mention the wide range of ecotheology and ecofeminist theology with early contributions by Jürgen Moltmann, Rosemary Radford Ruether, Sallie McFague, earlier still by Liberty Hyde Bailey and Joseph Sittler, later by Sigurd Bergmann, Mark I. Wallace, Catherine Keller, Whitney Bauman and many more.[5]

Michael Northcott supports White's interpretation, but only as long as it is limited to late medieval Latin Catholic theology. In Northcott's view, White completely overlooked the fact that the modern environmental move-ment—of which White himself was a part—has its roots in Protestantism.[6] Sociologist Bronislaw Szerszynski likewise complicates White's depiction by discussing whether the notion of nature as sacral is exhausted by the notion of nature as itself divine. Many scholars, he notes, have questioned whether nonmodern societies protected nature to any significant extent, and if they did so, was it necessarily due to spiritual beliefs?[7] Ecotheologian Celia Deane-Drummond becomes herself an example of Christian rethink-ing of the sacrality of nature mentioned by Szerszynski when arguing that, to her, a Christian life entails a nonanthropocentric move that enables critique of the works of man and the anthropogenic impact on the environment: a critique that calls the human community to care for and protect the earth.[8] Pope Francis similarly acknowledges that the Christian traditions are in part responsible for the current environmental situation, but also that Christians have a responsibility to return to their sources in light of the situation we are in.[9] In 2002, Pope John Paul II stated that an act of repentance is required, not only economically and technologically but also morally and spiritually. In fact, a passage in the Vatican's common declaration of environmental ethics echoes White's admonition, as outlined above. John Paul II writes:

> A solution at the economic and technological level can be found only if we undergo, in the most radical way, an inner change of heart, which can lead to a change in lifestyle and of unsustainable patterns

of consumption and production. A genuine *conversion* in Christ will enable us to change the way we think and act.[10]

The papal declaration underlines the humility that must arise from the recognition of the limits of human knowledge and judgement, but it still places man firmly at the centre of creation.[11] Thus, in their views of the central place given to humanity in creation, Pope John Paul II, Pope Francis and Celia Deane-Drummond alike do what White suggested Christians always have done: namely, they place humanity at the centre, which is why we are still caught in the very logic White suggested we need to rethink.

To some degree, humanity is naturally at the centre of most ecotheology—as it is for the present contribution—since the effort to preserve life on Earth generally implies not just any life but human life in particular.[12] Moreover, as theologian Jayne Svenungsson points out, the elevation of humanity in theology may also serve to remind us of our species' extraordinary destructive potential.[13] Still, there are differences in emphasis when it comes to the role of humanity, and White's article seems to bring the distinctions to the fore. Simply stated, either one approves of his critique and wants to think theology *with* it, or one is provoked and wants to think ecotheology *against* it. I consider either way promising since we need all the ecotheology we can get at this stage. If, however, one believes White has a point and feels that one's ecotheological reasoning has to take his critique into account, then the current contribution may be of assistance.

Mark I. Wallace's idea that the incarnation of Christ leads to God's incarnation in the material world is more in accord with the basic reasoning in White's article, since it describes the material world as such as divinity. To Wallace the world is the form God takes among us. The Earth is the body of the Spirit—hence humans violate God when they violate the Earth and each other. Humanity as the image of God is not to rise above the world but to acknowledge our earthliness. Or, expressed simply in Wallace's own words: "At one time, God was a bird".[14] Still, one may wonder, does it make a difference if God is described as a bird? Is God not somehow still the transcendent God, only in bird imagery? According to Clayton Crockett there are two basic problems that reoccur in many ecotheological approaches: First, he argues, the invocation of theological models of transcendence, in whatever form, inevitably devalues the world through the assumption that the world is not all there is. Why should a Christian finally care about the Earth if the Earth is not ultimate—if the bird is not really a bird but God, if it is not enough for a bird to be a bird? On the other hand, if a naturalistic understanding suffices to describe material life on Earth, why bother about religion? In Wallace's reasoning, Crockett states, the transcendent God merging with the Earth is nonetheless an attempt to retain God as a source of transcendent value that infuses the natural world. The natural world, in consequence, is situated within the spiritual play of Christianity, hence secondary to the spiritual world.[15] Second, Crockett argues, many ecotheologies appeal to a romanticised notion of the original human-nature relationship, whereas nature, he holds, "is not in a state of harmony; it does not exist or persist at equilibrium".[16] Many Christian responses to White's critique fall into the assumption that if we could only liberate the true essence of Christianity, we could restore the harmony on Earth.[17] In such responses, Crockett summarises, Christianity is what Plato calls the *pharmakon*—at once poison and potential cure.[18] Christianity is put forward as the problem and the solution, all in one.

In all honesty, does not any self-critical theology treat Christianity exactly thus—the present attempt and Crockett's contributions included? The point of critique and the level of harshness may differ, as may the solutions, but as long as one remains within the theological field, the Christian sources do play the role of the *pharmakon*. To me, that is not a problem. As a theological contribution, the current book is more concerned with creating new ways of thinking than about critiquing existing ways. Again, ecotheology of all kinds are needed because theology is a precarious business and the varieties of Christian faith require a plurality of voices.[19] Crockett gives voice to a scepticism shared by many, including me, and we do not have time to lose potential activists, thinkers, seekers, believers to a fruitless critical roundabout so let us generate more ways of thinking, believing and acting, so that more can be done. I agree with Donna Haraway that "we need a hardy, soiled kind of wisdom".[20] Like White, Pope John Paul II, Pope Francis and Deane-Drummond, Haraway cries out for change, but not one that will once more place either God or man at the centre—not one that advocates human responsibility—but rather one that points to multispecies *response-ability*.[21] Haraway is, together with Popova, our key thought companion in Chapter 2.

Ecotheologian Sigurd Bergmann employs the notion of *urban amnesia* to describe the forgetfulness of a place that enables its destruction. The fact that we so easily forget how it was—the grove where there now is a house—makes it easier for us to reshape and remould the world, he argues.[22] In his own work, Bergmann enters theology through art objects precisely because their concreteness helps him remember the spatial, the always material and contextual setting of life and of theology. Unlike many other theologians in the art and theology field, Bergmann therefore also engages with non-Western art. His analyses of Eastern Orthodox Christian imagery, of Greenlandic, Northern Swedish and Peruvian art entail a critique of a different form of spatial amnesia than the one just mentioned as that which enables the destruction of a place.[23] The spatial amnesia occurring when we forget the importance of space, of locality and the necessity of removing ourselves from our current position to get a new view. (Through the perspective of Vitor Westhelle, we discuss the notions of time and space further in Chapter 5.) Following Bergmann thus, would it make a difference if we, quite simply, searched elsewhere? If we invited a Russian thinker into the Western thought tradition, a thinker with a different locality in space and time? A thinker from a time in history—a time of scarcity and need—sharing our desperation for new ways of thinking and living, yet also from a cultural and theological sphere with a different history as regards the relationship between the material and the spiritual. Our next chapter looks deeper into that question but let me at this point invoke the figure with whom this project first set off.

Rethinking art with Liubov Popova

Ever since I first read the few theoretical contributions by Liubov Popova that accompany her rich artistic production, I have felt compelled to transmit her ideas in terms of a material theology for our time. Here is why I, a theologian, have left my comfort zone once again to introduce her artistic ideas to theology: First, Popova introduces an account of the artist's relation to the material world that combines a sense of possibility and trust in human creativity and technology with a deep humility in relation to the natural elements. Second, for this reason, her notion of the relationship between the artist and the material elements has not only ecological but also—primarily—political implications. By rethinking art, she imagines a new future society starting at the level of the everyday. Third, her approach to the elements of construction—the elements that make up this world—is inner-worldly yet spiritual. Her political determination, in other words, did not make her disregard the spiritual or enigmatic aspects of life and humanity, which is why she, as compared with many of her contemporaries and our contemporaries still today, stands forth as an unusually complex thinker. Fourth, the renegotiation of gender is a key part of her endeavour. By rethinking the notion of the artist, and calling herself a *constructor*, she destabilises not only the notion of art but also the gendered notion of the constructor—hence the idea of femininity. Finally, Popova was desperate for new ways of thinking—as are many of us—yet the historical picture in retrospect suggests that the collective despair of her dynamic generation of Russian thinkers should have been managed with greater caution. Though it is hard to detect seeds of totalitarianism at an early stage, it is imperative to try, and there are certainly aspects of Popova's thinking that remind us of where we should *not* go.

I first encountered Popova's art-theory perspectives when reading about Kazimir Malevich while writing my previous book, *Foucault, Art, and Radical Theology: The Mystery of Things*, and I felt that her contribution invited a next step. The book ended in a radical theology of marvels and actions. Following Foucault through art history, I sought to view the world as a surface of appearances—a surface with nothing beneath, yet in itself a plane of infinite complexity: the world seen as a surface instigating awe, humility and respect for difference; as a surface of knowledge, as a plane of words, expressions, things, narratives, gestures and identities making up reality as a mystery of things, a mystery that causes wonder. On the other hand, however, the mystery of things also instigates action. If expressions make up the world, why not take part in the expression-making, adding to the surface of appearances? Why not take part in forming knowledge as we know it, while realising we will never have the last word but always only the possibility to add and to reconstruct? This book starts where the last project ended—in a spirituality that is material and ready to act.

Popova was the starting point for this project, but as shall become evident the thinkers brought in as conversation partners—Donna Haraway, Walter Benjamin, Vitor Westhelle, Paul Tillich and Gilles Deleuze, to name a few—are just as important to the overall argument. Through materialist and constructivist thinkers of the twentieth century, we sketch the contours of a radical material theology leading to a manifesto of sorts. Why a manifesto? Because—in line with my reasoning on reality as a mystery of things—manifestos, statements and materialised words add truths to the multiplicity of reality. They make public what is already there, but mute. Manifestos hand a megaphone to the murmur, not in order to have the last say—the totality of manifestos is always plural—but to raise muted voices. In superficial profundity, playfully yet seriously, manifestos turn thoughts into things that matter. The manifesto format captures the energy and impatience of the constructivist movement as well as of the current awareness of planetary crisis. Yet a manifesto is always contingent. Simply by being stated, statements will be opposed. Placards decay, the paint flakes and fades, new placards are nailed over the old, hence every manifesto indicates a multiplicity of statements, and so does this one.

Popova and the life of construction

Is there a difference between technical creativity and artistic creativity? The question was implicitly posed by Paul Tillich in his 1952 lectures on art and society at the Minneapolis Institute of the Arts. Originally, he noted, the technical and the liberal arts were not separated; the fact that *Künstler* in German literally means "he who can", and that the Greek *poesis* is derived from *poiein*, making, producing, and that the Latin *ars* is the skill to fabricate something, indicates the original connection.[24] The separation between technical and artistic creativity occurred when tools became just tools—when a hammer was merely that with which you hammer, not an object of aesthetic quality.[25] Popova and her group of constructivists questioned that very separation, that is, the division between the technical and the liberal arts. In March 1921, the constructivists declared that they rejected easel painting to focus solely on creating objects for life, for the everyday life of a new Russian society. Popova joined them with a statement later that same year.[26] But let us take it from the beginning with a brief introduction to Popova's work and thought.

Liubov Popova (1889–1924)

Liubov Sergeyevna Popova was born in Ivanovskoe near Moscow in 1889 to a wealthy and cultured family, early on showing a strong interest in art—Italian Renaissance painting and Russian icons in particular—and taking art lessons from a young age. In the years 1907–1908 she entered the private studios of Stanislav Zhukovsky and Konstantin Youn in Moscow and was introduced to their mild form of impressionism.[27] In 1912–1913, when she attended the studios of Henri Le Fauconnier and Jean Metzinger in Paris, she had already begun to find her own pictorial language in the blossoming artistic life emerging in Russia at the time. She was inspired by French cubism and developed a cubist idiom of her own that became apparent in her work from those years. Popova and Nadezhda Udaltsova, both of whom had taken part in setting up a studio in Moscow, became members of the "Tower" studio organised by Vladimir Tatlin in autumn of 1912. By 1914–1916 she had become a key figure in the Russian avantgarde working with Udaltsova, Aleksandra Ekster and Olga Rozanova in significant exhibitions and organising weekly meetings with paper presentations in her home—attended by, among others, Pavel Florensky, whom we will encounter below.[28] She was also influenced by Islamic architecture, which struck her during a trip to Samarkand in 1916, and with her "painterly architectonics" series in 1916–1918 she moved on from cubist-futurist expressions towards the suprematist sphere.[29]

Suprematism, founded by Kazimir Malevich in 1915, can be described as a creation of the need for new forms of expression—even a new world—embodied in the revolutionary spirit of Russia at the time. Suprematism (from "supreme") refers to the notion of a nonobjective or abstract world beyond that of everyday reality. To Malevich, the forms in themselves as immaterial realities were the highest form of reality, holding a spiritual truth, and the artistic endeavour was a spiritual journey. There was a tension among the suprematists, however, between those who—like Malevich—saw art as a spiritual quest, and others who were more politically inclined, responding to the need for the artist to create a new physical world. Popova, as we shall see, embraced both these aims, but her political drive made her leave the suprematist circles for the constructivist—finally deciding to quit easel painting altogether.[30] Even during the short period when Popova was connected with the suprematist circles, her expression differed in crucial aspects from those of Malevich. Her work was less detached and, in that sense, less symbolic, more integrated into the space, material and colour of the composition, hence more architectural than metaphysical as compared with the work of Malevich.[31]

By the mid 1910s Popova was renowned, an undisputed artistic authority, yet her work has not been scrutinised by scholars as has that of colleagues like Vladimir Tatlin or Aleksandr Rodchenko, nor has it been discussed in relation to the branches of twentieth-century thought to which it has obvious connections. Her gender is likely one reason for the comparatively scarce critical attention, but another is the often-described incongruence of her contribution. On one hand, she was a materialist and political artist, yet on the other hand, she was a spiritual artist inspired not only by the Russian iconographic tradition, as many constructivists were, but also by the spirituality of suprematism and rayism.[32] She was, in that sense, not a hard-core constructivist—though, we should note with caution, attempting to delineate between and within the concurrent movements of the time is intricate, as the art-historical scholarship indicates.[33] What may be regarded as an incongruence from an art-historical perspective is a novel vantage point from a theological perspective, which is why the current study of her work attempts to speak where art historians have often remained silent. In this book we enter her work theologically at the intersection of the materialistic and the spiritual—an intersection that she shares with the thinkers who are brought in as conversation partners—entailing a move beyond representation

Disposition of the chapters

Chapter 1, delineating the backdrop, situates the contribution of this book within the field of art and theology in terms of building on and elaborating further the work of Paul Tillich and Mark C. Taylor. The theorists of Russian art and theology Clemena Antonova and Andrew Spira pave the way towards an Eastern rather than Western theology of art. My choice of Popova's constructivism as a source of theological inspiration suggests an Eastern-Western political theology with a twist.

In Chapter 2, Donna Haraway's "Manifesto for Cyborgs" meets Popova's renegotiation of the notions of art and the artist. The chapter focuses on a question addressed by both: What is creation and what is action if the borders between artist versus art, creator versus creation and human versus machine do not stand? And what is theology—activist theology in particular—if the distinction between creator and creation is dissolved? What could characterise a radical theology for cyborgs, an activist theology for constructors?

In Chapter 3, the Russian constructivist thought milieu is introduced by way of the constructivist focus on everyday objects. A comparison between Popova and Vladimir Tatlin is performed by way of Walter Benjamin. Benjamin's analytical tools throw light on the differences between Popova and Tatlin, and underline the enigmatic and spiritual aspects of things, matter and everyday objects in Popova's art and thought. On the basis of that analysis, the notion of *second theology* is introduced as a theological employment of Benjamin's notion of *second technology*. The chapter thus introduces second theology as an understanding of theology concurrent with the presuppositions of constructivism: a theology *of* construction and *under* construction.

Chapter 4 endeavours a second-theology construction by exploring a truly relational and material Christology when the notion of Christ as machine is suggested to complement the familiar image of Christ's face. With Deleuze and Guattari's machine concepts, as well as Haraway's critique of the abstract aspects of their thinking, we discuss an actual stage construction designed by Popova. We deal with questions such as what happens when ideas become tangible, when thoughts materialise and when humans and other species actually meet. The upshot is to suggest the image of Christ as machine, as a never-ending die-and-live-again-machine, moving through time and space as an ongoing repetition of difference. This is an understanding of Christ that nonetheless includes the face, as well as the early Christian symbol of the wheel.

Chapter 5 treats the notion of time as challenged by climate-change awareness and discusses Vitor Westhelle's notion of eschatology as spatial rather than temporal. Subsequently, an eschatology out of joint is explored through a Deleuzian interpretation of the Russian Orthodox notions of time and space that were already introduced in the backdrop, Chapter 1.

The conclusion is a manifesto summarising key points of the discussion yet, naturally, in its attempt to summarise it constructs something new.

Notes

1 Lynn White Jr., "The Historical Roots of Our Ecologic Crisis", *Science* 155, no. 3767 (10 March 1967), 1206.
2 White, "The Historical Roots of Our Ecologic Crisis", 1206.
3 Espeth Whitney, "Lynn White Jr.'s 'The Historical Roots of Our Ecological Crisis' After 50 Years", *Wiley Online Library*, 28 August 2015, https://doi.org /10.1111/hic3.12254; further examples are cited below.
4 Virginia Burrus notes that despite the fifty years of debate, the key arguments of White's article have never simply been dismissed or discarded. See Virginia Burrus, *Ancient Christian Ecopoetics: Cosmologies, Saints, Things* (Philadelphia: University of Pennsylvania Press, 2019).
5 For a fascinating journey through early contributions to ecotheology, see Panu Pihkala, *Early Ecotheology and Jospeh Sittler* (Zurich: LIT, 2017).
6 Referring to Mark Stoll, Belden Lane and Evan Berry, Northcott argues that "American environmentalism is clearly rooted in the Protestant, and more especially Presbyterian, tradition". He underlines that "all of the key figures in the conservation movement in nineteenth- and early twentieth-century America were raised Presbyterian including Emerson, Thoreau, Muir, Pinchot, Marsh and Roosevelt, and it is unsurprising that they made frequent use of biblical and Christian discourse in their arguments for the defence of nature". Michael Northcott, "Lynn White Jr. Right and Wrong: The Anti-Ecological Character of

Latin Christianity, and the Pro-Ecological Turn of Protestantism", in *Religion and Ecological Crisis: The "Lynn White Thesis" at 50*, eds. T. le Vasseur and A. Peterson (New York: Routledge, 2016), 61–74, 68. See also Michael Northcott, *The Environment and Christian Ethics* (Cambridge: Cambridge University Press, 1996).

7 Bronislaw Szerszynsky, *Nature, Technology and the Sacred* (Oxford: Blackwell, 2005), 35.

8 Drummond argues that "the experience of grace through the Holy Spirit active in the human community includes the determination to protect and care for the earth, ever groaning under the weight of (…) anthropogenic evils". Celia Deane Drummond, *Eco-Theology* (Winona: Saint Mary's Press, 2008), 180.

9 "If a mistaken understanding of our own principles has at times led us to justify mistreating nature, to exercise tyranny over creation, to engage in war, injustice and acts of violence, we believers should acknowledge that by so doing we were not faithful to the treasures of wisdom which we have been called to protect and preserve". Pope Francis, *Laudato Si: On Care for Our Common Home* (Vatican City: Vatican Press, 2015).

10 John Paul II, *Common Declaration of Environmental Ethics: Common Declaration of John Paul II and the Ecumenical Patriarch His Holiness Bartholomew I* (10 June 2002); www.vatican.va.

11 "A new approach and a new culture are needed, based on the centrality of the human person within creation". John Paul II, *Common Declaration of Environmental Ethics: Common Declaration of John Paul II and the Ecumenical Patriarch His Holiness Bartholomew I* (Monday, 10 June 2002); www.vatican.va.

12 Even though there are studies indicating that the survival of other species can have comforting functions in climate-change-related depressions, the survival of *any* life is not quite satisfactory to most eco-thinking and eco-activism. Robert Jay Lifton's term "symbolizing immortality" is frequently discussed in relation to this phenomenon. See Robert Jay Lifton, *The Protean Self: Human Resilience in an Age of Fragmentation* (Chicago: University of Chicago Press, 1993), and http://www.tidskriftenikaros.fi/artikel/klimatangest-som-en-forandrande-kraft/.

13 Jayne Svenungsson, "Interdependence and the Biblical Legacy of Anthropocentrism: On Human Destructiveness and Human Responsibility", in *Eco-Ethica, OnlineFirst* (August 8, 2018).

14 Mark I. Wallace, *When God Was a Bird: Christianity, Animism, and the Re-Enchantment of the World* (New York: Fordham University Press, 2019), i. See also Clayton Crockett, "Earth", in *An Insurrectionist Manifesto: Four New Gospels for a Radical Politics*, eds. Ward Blanton, Clayton Crockett, Jeffrey W Robbins, and Noëlle Vahanian (New York: Columbia University Press, 2016), 33.

15 Crockett, "Earth", 34.

16 Ibid.

17 Crockett, "Earth", 33.

18 Ibid.

19 In *Beyond Monotheism*, Laurel C. Schneider sketches the many beginnings of Christianity and the multiplicity of Christian monotheisms. She quotes Mark Jordan who puts it succinctly: "Theology not written as a life told four ways already departs from the most authoritative model for Christian writing". Laurel C. Schneider, *Beyond Monotheism: A Theology of Multiplicity* (New York: Routledge, 2008), 8.

20 Donna Haraway, *Staying with the Trouble: Making Kin in the Chthulucene* (Durham: Duke University Press, 2016), 110.
21 Haraway, *Staying with the Trouble*, 110.
22 Sigurd Bergmann, *Religion, Space and the Environment* (New York: Routledge, 2017), 87–93.
23 Sigurd Bergmann, *In the Beginning is the Icon: A Liberative Theology of Images, Visual Arts and Culture* (London: Routledge, 2016), discusses the Christian tradition of iconography and its relationship to material reality as an opening for a what Bergmann names a liberative theology.
24 Paul Tillich, "Lecture 2: Culture, Society, and Art", trans. Robert P. Scharlemann, in *Paul Tillich on Art and Architecture*, eds. John Dillenberger and Jane Dillenberger (New York: Crossroad, 1987), 21–31, 24.
25 Tillich observes: "Tools became mere tools, determined exclusively by their use, and artistic activity liberated itself from union with technical production and created the arts as an independent sphere of culture" (Tillich, "Lecture 2: Culture, Society, and Art", 24.
26 Liubov Popova, untitled manuscript, signed and dated December 1921, manuscript department at State Tretiakov Gallery, Moscow (fond 148, op.17, l. 3–4). Cited in Christina Lodder, "Liubov Popova: From Painting to Textile Design", in *Tate Papers*, no. 14 (Autumn 2010); https://www.tate.org.uk/research/publica tions/tate-papers/14/liubov-popova-from-painting-to-textile-design, accessed 3 January 2019.
27 Tom Sandqvist, *Det andra könet i öst: Om kvinnliga konstnärer i den central- och östeuropeiska modernismen* (Stockholm: Symposium, 2010), 114.
28 M. N. Yablonskaya, *Women Artists of Russia's New Age: 1900–1935* (London: Thames and Hudson, 1990), 102; see also Sandqvist, *Det andra könet i öst*, 116.
29 Yablonskaya, *Women Artists of Russia's New Age*, 104; Dmitri V. Sarabianov, "Painting", in *Liubov Popova*, eds. Dimitri V. Sarabianov and Natalia L. Adaskina, trans. Marian Schwartz (New York: Abrams, 1990), 12–147, 109, 134.
30 Lodder argues that while the difference between the spiritually oriented suprematism and the politically oriented constructivism is palpable, it should not be overstated; the similarities were many, she argues, and remained so throughout the existence of the two movements. See Christina Lodder, "Conflicting Approaches to Creativity? Suprematism and Constructivism", in *Celebrating Suprematism: New Approaches to Kazimir Malevich*, ed. Christina Lodder (Leiden: Brill, 2019), 259–288, 260.
31 Yablonskaya, *Women Artists of Russia's New Age*, 103–104. Sarabianov suggests that "Suprematism did act as a kind of stimulus, a catalyst in Popova's art, but it never became her 'native language'" (Sarabianov, "Painting", 111).
32 Sandqvist simply calls her "eclectic" (Sandqvist, *Det andra könet i öst*, 115). See also Diana Kaur and Padraic E. Moore, *Nevertheless, Faith is in the Air: A Treatise on the Existence of True Faith in the 21st Century via an Analysis of Seven Artworks from the Collection of Moderna Museet* (Stockholm: Moderna Museet, 2010), 433494437. (Yes, the page number is correct; this wonderfully experimental little book has adopted a mysterious mathematical system for its pagination.)
33 Laurel Fredrickson both summarises and criticises the attempts at labelling the different fractions of constructivism referring to the work of Christina Lodder, Paul Overy and Larissa Alekseevna Zhadova. See Fredrickson, "Vision and Material Practice", 51, 71.

1   The backdrop

Theology of art from Tillich to Popova

When German theologian and forerunner of radical theology Dorothee Sölle met the Jewish religious thinker Martin Buber in Israel in the wake of the Second World War, she is said to have introduced herself as a theologian, to which Buber responded: "Theology—how do you do that?" At that moment of postwar devastation, when the very notion of speaking (*logos*) of God was rent to pieces, Buber's question cut to the heart of Sölle's struggle. She then spent her entire academic career exploring a theology that was operational and socially brave, only seldom using the term theologian to describe herself.[1] "I need to ground heaven on earth", Sölle wrote in 1993.[2] To her, theology was about analysing real-life circumstances. As theologians we should look deep into lived reality, she argued, until we "reach a point where theological reflection becomes necessary".[3] Theologians must "read the context until it cries out for theology".[4]

The field of "theology and art" is growing while the world is burning. Is that a sign of escapism on the part of theology—is theology hiding out in art museums and galleries? Or is the escapism on the part of art—is the art world seeking comfort in the chapel? Neither, in my view; escapism is not the reason for the trend on either side. Rather, on the contrary, the growing interest in art and theology today is related to the issue addressed by Buber and Sölle: How do we actually *do* theology? How does theology become materially and politically active, relevant and concrete? How do we ground heaven on earth? Rather than being a sign of escapism, I am persuaded that theology's turn to art is responding to the fact that it is concrete and bears political import without diminishing the enigmatic aspects of reality. The following discussion introduces only a fraction of the rich field of theology and art, but one indicating the sources and the direction of the current contribution: We move from Tillich's theology of art to Eastern iconographic theology and then to Russian political art. Tillich's focus on the meaning of existence, which may have been key in his time, is not necessarily in ours, which is why the current project turns to other more contemporary sources. And yet we begin with Tillich because his notion of God as ultimate concern—even beyond the revelation of Christian dogma—paved the way for the reconstruction and deconstruction still characterising the field. We then move to Clemena Antonova and Andrew Spira's views on the theological dimensions of the Russian pictorial space. Finally, we turn to Popova's politically oriented yet spiritually informed constructivism. Against the backdrop of Tillich, Taylor and Russian iconographic theology, I indicate why Popova's constructivist approach is an apt source for radical material theology to be explored in the chapters to come.

Tillich's concrete concern

Paul Tillich offered the most ambitious attempt of the twentieth century to bridge the Western divide between art as a secular enterprise and theology. His theological engagement with art exceeds that of any other theologian of his generation and reaches beyond his engagement with art in his writing, lecturing and as curator.[5] Without Tillich's theory of correlation, as Russell Re Manning observes, we might not have seen the now established area of study denoted as "theology and the arts" in countless undergraduate courses in theology.[6] Without Tillich, in consequence, it is likely this book would never have been written. Through his theological, philosophical and cultural analyses he introduced a language that enabled a genuine dialogue with the arts, both in terms of theology's interpretation of art and in terms of art's impact on theological development.[7]

To what extent did Tillich's art analyses truly enter into the artistic domain of thought, however, and into a genuine dialogue with the arts? Or, to frame it differently, to what extent did he manage to bridge the divide between the material and the spiritual? To many, Tillich is the ontotheologian *par excellence*, hence his search for meaning in artworks necessarily strives beyond, and finally disregards, the material composition as such. Rather than bridging the material-versus-spiritual divide, Tillich appears to detach art from its material aspects and extract only its "spiritual" content when relating it to theology. When art meets theology in Tillich's thinking, it has already turned immaterial. Extending Buber's question, noted above, one may ask: Is Tillich's theology of art, despite its concrete object, a theology that *is* rather than a theology that *does*—a theology of *being* rather than of *doing*?

According to Tillich's general understanding of culture, it consists of three elements: *Form* (form), *Inhalt* (content) and *Gehalt* (substance). While Tillich emphasises that all three are related, dependent on and intertwined with each other, he also formulates a general principle according to which "the more *Form*, the more autonomy; the more *Gehalt*, the more theonomy".[8] In other words, Tillich locates the theologically relevant aspects of cultural expressions ("the theonomy") to their substance understood as their meaning or import, not to their form nor even to their content as such. An artwork's substance—its inner nucleus or character, not its material form—may disclose a matter of ultimate concern, may direct its viewers towards "the ultimate reality beyond everything that seems to be real", towards "being-itself" as "the power of being in everything that is".[9] The very materiality of art, art materialised as form, on the other hand, leads to *autonomy* which according to Tillich's general rule, is the opposite of theonomy or even the opposite of a correlation between religion and culture. Hence the relevance of my question; to what extent did Tillich enter into an artistic domain of thought? If finally disregarding the form, and separating form from substance of meaning to focus primarily on the latter, what becomes of the actual objects of art? Has art not, in Tillich's systematic theological thinking, turned into an immaterial or even spiritual essence—a spiritual, cultural essence that is understood as opposed to a material, natural object?

In his essay "Changing Ontotheology: Paul Tillich, Catherine Malabou, and the Plastic God", Jeffrey Robbins uses the passage quoted above to show how much of an ontotheologian Tillich really is.[10] Robbins argues that for Tillich the final reality, the really real, is not the material level of life— not the surface of appearances—but the ground of all levels, being-itself. Or, as in another passage by Tillich:

> In our search for the 'really real' we are driven from one level to another to the point where we cannot speak of level anymore, where we must ask for that which is the ground of all levels, giving them their structure and their power of being. The search for ultimate reality beyond everything that seems to be real is the search for being-itself, for the power of being in everything that is.[11]

The ontotheological account appears presupposed in the very idea of a theory of correlation and the way it analyses the dialectic of *Form-Inhalt-Gehalt* using the notions of cultural form versus religious content.[12] The idea of detecting religious content or substance in secular-cultural form presupposes a separation between form and content, hence a separation between matter and spirit—a distinguishability between an object's appearance and its inner substance. In this perspective, the current project stands forth as Tillich's theological opposite. Contrary to Tillich, the current project attempts to ground a radical theology in artistic material techniques and actions—and in form. The form versus matter distinction shall be further discussed by way of Popova in the chapters to come but let us not leave Tillich just yet because there is reason to revisit Tillich on this point.

In an unpublished paper, architecture and philosophy scholar David Capener argues that there is an often overlooked and more material Tillich that the notion of the ontotheologian overshadows, and I owe the following nuanced view of Tillich to Capener. Because, as John Clayton observes, when approaching the dialectic of *Form-Inhalt-Gehalt* in Tillich's thinking "we plunge into those dark depths of Tillich's thought where, if not all, certainly most of the cows are black".[13] The distinctions Tillich proposes are, on a closer look, not in fact distinctions at all but fractions, elements of a unity that is not necessarily a singular unity but may just as well be understood as a multiple whole. John Thatamanil argues that the description of Tillich as ontotheologian obscures the complexity of Tillich's notion of being. He reads Tillich as a theologian of finitude, matter and potentiality.[14] Even if Tillich does describe being-itself as the ground of all levels, that ground—being—remains shrouded in mystery. Being for Tillich is at once *Grund* and *Ungrund*, ground as well as abyss, which is why Tillich's God as being-itself somewhat dialectically includes both being and nonbeing.[15] As foundation, Tillich's being destabilises every foundation. Donald F. Dreisbach even underlines that the dialectic between being and nonbeing, and between essence and existence, is essential to Tillich's notion of the possibilities of life. In Tillich's view *to be* is to actualise potentialities, Dreisbach argues, hence, *to be* is necessarily also to become a distortion of one's essential nature. One's essence and thus one's potentialities remain, but as existing one manifests them in an incomplete and distorted way. In other words, to affirm existence is unavoidably also to affirm nonexistence, it is to affirm finitude as the very condition of life. Life as such is always situated and always limited or else it is not living. In Tillich's own words:

> An expression of man's finitude is his necessity to dwell, to have a place. He is excluded from the infinite space and, even if he pushes into it without a definite limit to the farthest stars, he must start in a definite place and return to another definite place.[16]

Similarly, for Tillich God as the ultimate concern, as being itself, is concrete: "The ultimate concern is a concrete concern; otherwise it could not be a concern at all".[17] It is expressed in an actual religion and is in that sense material, not idealistic.

In a 1948 sermon entitled "Nature, Also, Mourns for a Lost Good", Tillich expresses what may be regarded as an ecotheological argument based on the materiality of Christian sacramentality and the incarnational thought structure. Artists, Tillich suggests, have often understood the religious significance of nature better than theologians who more often tend to assume a bodiless spirituality. And yet, he continues, the sacramental is the union of the sacred and the profane, the spiritual and the material, why nature—not just *creation* as a Christian concept, but the actual "stars and the clouds, the winds and the oceans, the stones and the plants, the animals and our own bodies"—is pivotal to Christian faith.[18] "Therefore", Tillich finally exclaims, "commune with nature! Become reconciled with nature after your estrangement from it".[19] This is to affirm, then, that it is not my intention to disregard Tillich's contribution to the theology of art and to radical material theology, but to explore further the field he initiated by moving the theological emphasis from *Gehalt* to *Form* onto the materiality of art, and life.

Objects of not-knowing

Mark C. Taylor continued Tillich's theological work on art and enacted an even more thorough analysis of modern art from his a/theological perspective. In *Disfiguring* (1992) he created a dialogue between modern art, architecture and theology. Taylor's a/theological perspective, in his own words, "explores the middle ground between classic theology and atheism", an in-between of interstitial space and intermediate time. He develops an a/theological-philosophical argument to establish implicit as well as explicit spiritual preoccupations of key twentieth-century artworks. I have argued elsewhere, however, that Taylor's interstitial space and intermediate time never fully take place, that they do not situate themselves.[20] Taylor's journey through twentieth-century art is a journey through deconstructive "fragments of knowledge", "ruins of words", "demise of writing"—not fragments of *matter*, not ruins of *buildings*, not demise of *living bodies*.[21] Looking back, I now believe it was partly unfair to suggest that his analyses lacked a sense of thingness given that he certainly does dwell in places, in front of paintings and architecture. He lets his readers relate to objects together with him, he circles around buildings and art objects, and his analyses arise from concrete observations. Still, in the end it has to do with knowledge, with logos, with the word—a scattered knowledge, a not-knowing, hence a logos turned silent and a word fragmented. Knowledge, logos and word are at the centre of attention and analysis, not the material world. Thus, the examples of Tillich and Taylor both illustrate what is suggested in the introduction; namely, that early radical theology was more focused on epistemology and linguistics than on politics and materiality. For good reasons, radical theology deconstructed the very notion of Christian knowledge and truth from the 1960s onwards, but now I believe it is time to add the action. Existence is threatened, which is why we explore new sources for a radical material theology that is political and ecological—a radical theology that *acts*, that *does*.

Naturally, any theoretical work ends in an abstract argument no matter how concrete the study material, yet the theological analyses of art theorists Clemena Antonova and Andrew Spira differ from those of Tillich and Taylor; in their analyses, the materiality of art is not secondary to Christian truth, but rather the latter is inseparable from the former. Christian truths are situated in the very artistic techniques and artefacts. Is it because they, unlike Tillich and Taylor, are art theorists and thus enter their analyses from a different angle? Or, is it because they deal with Eastern Christian rather than Western Christian art? Antonova's *Space, Time and Presence in the Icon* (2009) suggests the latter. The painting technique of Russian iconography inspired Popova and the Russian avantgarde in general—Vladimir Tatlin even trained as an icon painter.[22] Art historian John Milner suggests that for the avantgarde the icon provided a Russian alternative to Western traditions, one that placed an emphasis on the materials as well as on the refined painting technique, and according to Antonova this artistic technique conveys an at-times neglected aspect of Orthodox doctrine.[23] Antonova's view of the icon-painting technique introduces a Russian Orthodox thought-world that influenced Popova and her fellow constructivists, and since we shall discuss a twisted version of Antonova's reasoning in Chapter 4, let me outline her argument here.

Western viewing habits

Antonova argues that Western viewers of medieval Russian icons often assume a Western post-Renaissance pictorial logic when trying to understand them. In Russian medieval icons, frontal and profile aspects of the same object are often depicted alongside each other. To later Western viewers this is generally perceived as a "distorted" use of perspective, and scholars have drawn attention to the connections between cubism, especially early analytical cubism, and medieval iconography in this regard.[24] Antonova too sees and discusses the connections, but her analysis also makes clear that what is a distortion of habitual viewing patterns in Western modern art could in fact be a straightforward theological depiction of reality in Eastern iconography. Many explanations of the medieval phenomenon have been suggested ever since Oskar Wulff's article "Die umgekehrte Perspektive und die Niedersicht" ("Reverse Perspective") in 1907—none of them satisfactory to Antonova, however, who instead suggests a specific Russian Orthodox lens is needed to understand the pictorial space of the icon with its reverse perspective.[25] As long as a linear three-dimensional perspective is assumed the pictorial space will not make sense, she argues, because space in icon art is much more complex.[26] A Western viewer of a painting in which, say, the front of a church building would be seen alongside the left side of the building, would see the image as a distortion of reality since reality from a Western post-Renaissance point of view begins with the viewing subject. The linear three-dimensional perspective in depiction assumes a viewing subject as the key point of reference to reality. If the pictorial space does not make sense from a singular viewpoint, it either makes no sense at all or alters sense altogether. But for Antonova the Orthodox thought tradition opens an altogether different perspective, one she finds expressed in the writings by Pavel Florensky.

Florensky, who wrote an in-depth analysis of Picasso's construction of pictorial space in his paintings of musical instruments, uses the term "supplementary planes" to describe the fact that angles that would be obscured to the viewer are nevertheless depicted in the icon as well as in Picasso's cubist paintings.[27] Like many of his generation, Florensky was acquainted with the theosophical movement, hence it is likely that the theosophical notions of "transparent vision" or "synthetic vision" and the "fourth dimension" are present in Florensky's notion of the supplementary planes.[28] From a theosophical perspective, an object depicted as showing many planes at once on the pictorial plane would be interpreted as perceived from a higher viewpoint—the point of view of the "astral vision" on the "astral plane", a gaze obtainable only for the spiritually mature.[29]

To Antonova, however, though Florensky may have been more indebted to theosophical ideas than he cared to admit, it is just as likely that the ideas he encountered in the theosophical movement merely concurred with aspects of the Orthodox theology in which he was already immersed. Antonova holds that there is a structural analogy between the artistic principle of the "supplementary planes" of the icon—and of cubism for that matter—and the theological notion of a timelessly eternal, simultaneously existing God.[30] The icon may very well depict the world not from the viewpoint of a spiritually mature human being but from the viewpoint of a timeless God. She explains:

> A being who exists beyond time and, implicitly, beyond space and who, therefore, has no point of view, would perceive all aspects of an object in our world simultaneously, that is, in a manner similar to that described by the principle of 'supplementary planes'.[31]

In the writings on the Holy Spirit by Basil of Caesarea (329–379 CE), she argues, God's eternity is to be understood precisely as timeless, beyond time. For Gregory Nazianzen (330–389 CE), similarly, God is negatively defined through timelessness: "that which is temporal is not God".[32]

Pseudo-Dionysius the Areopagite reinforces this further by stating that eternal things should not be regarded as coeternal with God because God precedes eternity. God is not everlasting *in* time but is *before* time, *outside* of time, is even "the cause of all time and eternity".[33] Beyond time there is no division, no future, no present, no past—all is present and visible at once. The same idea is reflected in the Orthodox liturgy, Antonova argues, where the use of present and future tenses is illogical as long as time is understood in terms of linearity. To state that the Virgin "today gives birth to him" who, in turn, is to be born "tomorrow", yet "today" is showing himself, is of course confusing if one expects a Christian linearity of a past origin, a present and a future eschatological hope.[34] While the linear notion of time is present in the idea of Christianity as a history of salvation, liturgical time, by contrast, is cyclical. In the liturgy the world is created now, it ends now, God dies now, God rises now and Jesus is born now. If liturgical time is understood through the notion of a timeless eternity—that is, a simultaneous divine existence that contains all time in itself—the liturgical understanding of temporality changes even further. The once-and-for-all event of Christ's death and resurrection is no longer a *once-then* event for all future events, but an *all-at-once* phenomenon in a world finally resting on timelessness. Every stage of what we experience as a history of salvation is right there, present before the eyes of God. Analogically, an icon depicting the world as perceived by God is not viewed from a particular viewpoint in time and space but is experienced from every angle at once. Thus, the icon technique requires the supplementary planes where the world is viewed not from a singular viewpoint but from many viewpoints simultaneously—or is even, as Fabian Heffermehl argues, seen from within as a place of presence from which the world appears. Not as an optic vision, but as a haptic presence. Not as something to be viewed at a distance, but something to be felt in its immediacy as a complex and mysterious expression of God's incarnation.[35] The icon is thus always iconoclastic, Heffermehl holds, since it destroys from within our idea of an image as something to be viewed from without. In front of an icon that shows several angles at once, the viewer need not walk around, viewing first the front, then the side, in a linear viewing process of beginning, middle and end, but views as from a timeless point where all is immediately present.

Heffermehl does in fact critique Antonova's understanding of the reversed perspective in medieval iconography since he finds the notion of perspective as such problematic when superimposed on a medieval understanding of icons. The medieval Russian icon, understood in relation to the *acheiropoiesis* principle, he reasons, is not an image but precisely an icon in which the one depicted is present, presented, rather than merely re-presented. Yet, in Heffermehl's view Florensky makes the same mistake. Antonova and

Florensky alike understand the reversed perspective anachronistically by viewing the icon as an object (viewed from without) rather than a subject (viewed from within). I find, however, that Heffermehl slightly exaggerates the external perspective in Antonova's reasoning; what she describes is a perspective from a spaceless and timeless point, hence not external in any plain sense.

For Antonova, the liturgical distortion of time similarly indicates that the death of Christ is not a once-and-for-all event within the linearity of time but an ongoing event in the present, and so likewise is the eschatological event, and the creation of the world. If God is understood as timelessness, then the divine viewpoint becomes spatial rather than temporal: spatial not in terms of being located, but spatiality understood in its totality, conceived not as extension but as tangible presence.

Through Antonova's journey in the landscape of Eastern Orthodox art and theology the divine appears as the atemporal foundation of reality. Paradoxically, the presupposition of atemporality enables the material and the spatial to stand forth in their immediate presence, as her argument concerning the all-at-once character of both Orthodox liturgy and Orthodox icon art makes clear. The death of Christ as an ongoing liturgical event, recurrently repeated, multiplying itself endlessly. As such, it is a death without a first, without an origin, since it is situated at once in the present and beyond—or before—time as such. The icon image presents its entire materiality at once without having to rely on a singular viewing subject in order to make sense. The world is not presented so as to make sense from the human point of view; it is not there to serve human rationality. In the world of Russian iconography and liturgy Man is not the centre of reality.

Still, as noted, the spatiality Antonova describes is one without locality; the timeless God is also a spaceless God, and to that extent transcendent in the true sense of the word. Is it not in that sense a God far from Sölle's attempt to ground heaven on earth? Far from her idea that theology should start in the local, in the lived context, and far from the present endeavour commencing in our threatened existence on our worn-down planet? As the cause of time—as the very ground of temporal and spatial existence—the Eastern Christian God introduced through Antonova even resembles Tillich's ground of being. God as the basis of existence, beyond or beneath time and space. Moreover, the distortion of any single human point of view in icon art, the multiple and thus nonsensical perspective, instigates a human "not-knowing" similar to the desert in which Mark C. Taylor left us in *Disfiguring*. In God's perspective the world does not make human sense. While Antonova points to the concrete painting technique to discover a theological perspective, what she finally finds—the divinity that it points towards—is that not anything but material and timely? Clayton Crockett notes that when the temporal and spatial reality on Earth is placed within the spiritual play of Christianity, our planet world inevitably becomes secondary to the spiritual world.[36] Yet we can ask whether that is necessarily so, or would it make a difference if the spiritual is haptic—something to be felt rather than viewed or thought? The immediate presence that renders time and space chaotic—is that really a transcendent unity in the way we habitually regard transcendent unity?

Unity and diversity

There are different trajectories within the Russian avantgarde. Even though Popova is inspired by medieval iconography and spends a few years working in the circles of Malevich, and while Florensky is one of the attendees of the weekly discussions in her home, Popova does not choose the spiritual path described above as related to platonic ideas of art but instead moves on to the material and political constructivist movement.[37] Andrew Spira's account of the influence of iconography in Popova's art is telling of the transition we choose to make theologically when we follow Popova rather than the more explicitly spiritual trajectories of the Russian avantgarde. Following Popova theologically means not to leave Antonova's important insights behind but possibly to twist them slightly. It means bringing to bear the materiality and multiplicity of Russian iconography and Orthodox liturgy but letting go of the transcendent One as habitually understood, and to note instead the plurality of perspectives contained in the transcendent gaze in the materiality of spatial and temporal reality. It is to bring God down to Earth where the viewpoints are necessarily dispersed and scattered—a multiple God as a compound transcendence on the face of the Earth.

In *The Avant-Garde Icon* (2008), Spira treats the relationship between the Russian avantgarde and the icon tradition, noting that Popova's early interest in icons was more and more noticeable as she matured as a painter. Her "painterly architectonics" series from the years 1916–1918 conveyed a move away from cubist-futurism, and to Spira this is also a development that renders visible an iconographic inspiration. Popova had been impressed by Mikhail Vrubel's frescos in St. Cyril Church in Kiev and made visits to several centres of medieval icon painting in Russia such as Novogrod, Pskov, Suzdal, Yaroslavl and Rostov the Great.[38] Like many of her generation—including Olga Rozanova, Mikhail Larinov and Natalia Goncharova—Popova only began using this early source of inspiration once she had found her own pictorial language. What Spira describes as "a truly iconic dimension" of her work appears only when she has relaxed her dependence on the cubist language. Only then appears "the sense of monumentality, grandeur and composure" that, for Spira, truly signals the icon inspiration.[39] While

I agree with Spira that Popova's painterly architectonics more confidently occupies the canvas than her earlier cubist work, thus expressing a sense of grandeur and composure at once, I find another aspect of her icon inspiration more pertinent and more interesting for my purposes here. Spira's discussion of *Christ in Majesty* (c. 1500) in the city of Rostov the Great stresses the iconographic meaning of geometrical shapes, and his reasoning resembles Antonova's treatment, discussed above. The significance of geometrical shapes in icons is not merely symbolic, Spira states, but stems from an old tradition of understanding the complexity of the phenomenal world by seeing it in terms of the coherent numerical relationships that inform it. All numbers multiply and modify the number one, the unity that makes up the common subsistence. The regularity of the diverse shapes points towards that unity.[40] Spira notes an equivalence to this unity-in-diversity in one of

Figure 1.1 Painterly Architectonics (1916)

Popova's paintings in the *Painterly Architectonics* series in which, Spira states, "the diversity of energy is united in the coherence of its relationships and in the singularity of its aesthetic impact".[41] Spira suggests that the different geometrical shapes in Popova's paintings, while striving in different directions—the black square enlarged, stretched out diagonally, and the lighter black and the red hidden, almost disappearing beneath the expanded black—nonetheless constitute a congruent and harmonious whole as painterly composition (or "construction", as Popova would eventually prefer to call it).[42] There is, in short, a unity of diversity in Popova's painting just as in the icon *Christ in Majesty*.

For the purpose of the current book, the difference between the compositions is as interesting as what unites them. Exploring the political potential of radical theology's trajectory, we reach for a theology beyond that notion of political theology that remains dependent on the sovereign force understood as the One. We turn to art because it is concrete, hands on, and inspires theology to be likewise—a doing rather than a being. And yet, thus far, the One appears to be precisely what we find. According to Spira, the number one is the common subsistence of every form, every energy in the *Christ in Majesty* icon, a unity that parallels the coherence uniting the diversity of energy in Popova's painterly architectonics. Comparing the two, in turn, to the timeless transcendent God that enables the multiplicity of perspectives and times in icon art and in Orthodox liturgy as understood by Antonova, God, the transcendent one in her analysis, has a similar function of uniting diversity. In all three examples, the abstract unity beyond the concrete diversity is what enables the multiplicity, the different energies, the many angles and times. Or is it? Is there not a difference between Popova's unity of diversity and that of the iconography in this regard? Or, is there perhaps less of a unity in the iconographic technique itself than Spira suggests—a technique later deployed by the constructivists? Latvian painter and art theorist Voldemars Matvejs, an influential intellectual in the Russian avantgarde at the time, praised the icon precisely for *resisting* the will to unify. The icon mixes high and low, it allows a heterogeneity of colour and materials—hence a material noise—that modern oil painting silences, he reasoned. The icon, for Matvejs, is not unifying at all but suggests a way for art to allow the noisiness of its very materiality.[43]

Popova recurrently states that she aims to move beyond representational art in every sense of the term. Even the distorted faces of cubism are finally too caught up with depicting reality as if there were an origin, a unity, a given to depict, she argues. Or rather, regardless of whether there is a given, to represent the given is not the artistic task. *Expediency* is what Popova is seeking in the early 1920s, not aesthetics, not depiction of unity or of anything at all.[44] Expediency, (*tselesoobraznost*) meaning purposiveness, functionality, literally "formed in relation to a goal" is an often-used concept among the Russian constructivists at the time. Popova has no time for representing the past, representing the origin, representing truth, styles, ideals, because she needs to construct a liveable future society, she needs an art that functions, that *does* something rather than just *is*. But how is that to be done? What is agency, creation and creativity if the origin and the perspective of the viewer are replaced with a pluriform and haptic present? Let us find out by letting Popova encounter Donna Haraway.

Notes

1 Sarah K. Pinnock, ed., *The Theology of Dorothee Sölle* (Harrisburg: Trinity Press International, 2003), 71–72.
2 Dorothee Sölle, *On Earth as in Heaven: A Liberation Spirituality of Sharing* (Louisville: Westminster John Knox, 1993), ix.
3 Ibid.
4 Ibid.
5 Russell Re Manning, "Tillich's Theology of Art", in *The Cambridge Companion to Paul Tillich*, ed. Russell Re Manning (Cambridge: Cambridge University Press, 2009), 152–172.
6 Ibid., 154.
7 Ibid., 152.
8 Russell Re Manning, *Theology at the End of Culture: Paul Tillich's Theology of Culture and Art* (Leuven: Peeters, 2005), 117.
9 Paul Tillich, *Biblical Religion and the Search for Ultimate Reality*, 1st ed. (Chicago: University of Chicago Press, 1955), 13.
10 Jeffrey W. Robbins, "Changing Ontotheology: Paul Tillich, Catherine Malabou, and the Plastic God", in *Retrieving the Radical Tillich: His Legacy and Contemporary Importance*, ed. Russell Re Manning (New York: Palgrave Macmillan, 2015), 159–77, 159.
11 Paul Tillich, *Biblical Religion and the Search for Ultimate Reality*, 1st ed. (Chicago: University of Chicago Press, 1964), 13.
12 John Powell Clayton, *The Concept of Correlation: Paul Tillich and the Possibility of a Mediating Theology* (New York: de Gruyter, 1980), 191.
13 Ibid.
14 John Thatamanil, "Tillich and the Postmodern", in *The Cambridge Companion to Paul Tillich*, ed. Russell Re Manning (Cambridge: Cambridge University Press 2009), 288–302.
15 David Capener made this observation on Tillich and the material, then generously handed the ideas over to me when deciding to dig into the work of Henri Lefebvre instead. Thanks, David!
16 Paul Tillich, "Lecture 2: Culture, Society, and Art", trans. Robert P. Scharlemann, in *Paul Tillich on Art and Architecture*, eds. John Dillenberger and Jane Dillenberger (New York: Crossroad, 1987), 24.
17 Paul Tillich, "The Problem of Theological Method (1947)", in *Paul Tillich: Main Works 4, Writings in the Philosophy of Religion*, ed. John Clayton (New York: de Gruyter, 1987), 301–312, 304.
18 Panu Pihkala, *Early Ecotheology and Joseph Sittler* (Zürich: LIT Verlag, 2017), 171.

19 Ibid., 173.
20 Petra Carlsson, "Foucault, Velazquez and the Place of Theology", *Studia Theologica: Nordic Journal of Theology* 69, no. 2 (2015): 126–149.
21 Mark C. Taylor, *Disfiguring: Art, Architecture, Religion* (Chicago: Chicago University Press, 1992), 270.
22 See, for example, Louise Hardiman and Nicola Kozicharow, "Introduction", in *Modernism and the Spiritual in Russian Art: New Perspectives*, eds. Louise Hardiman and Nicola Kozicharow (Cambridge: Open Books, 2017), 9–36, 9; Laurel Fredrickson, "Vision and Material Practice: Vladimir Tatlin and the Design of Everyday Objects", *Design Issues* 15, no. 1 (Spring 1999): 49–74, 55.
23 See John Milner, *Vladimir Tatlin and the Russian Avantgarde* (New Haven: Yale University Press, 1983).
24 Argyro Loukaki, *The Geographical Unconscious* (New York: Routledge, 2014), 127; Robert Nelson, *The Spirit of Secular Art: A History of the Sacramental Roots of Contemporary Artistic Values* (Clayton: Monash University Epress, 2007), 08,10.
25 Oskar Wulff, *Die umgekehrte Perspektive und die Niedersicht: eine Raumanschauungsform der altbyzantinischen Kunst und ihre Fortbildung in der Renaissance* (1907); cited by Clemena Antonova, "On the Problem of 'Reverse Perspective': Definitions East and West", *Leonardo* 43, no. 5 (2010): 464–469.
26 Antonova, "On the Problem of 'Reverse Perspective'", 466.
27 See Pavel Florensky, "Reverse Perspective", in *Beyond Vision: Essays on the Perception of Art*, ed. Nicoletta Misher, trans. Wendy Salmond (London: Reaktion, 2002), 201. Florensky writes on Picasso in "The meaning of Idealism", 1914; the article is only available in Russian according to Antonova, *Space, Time and Presence in the Icon*, 113.
28 Antonova, *Space, Time, and Presence in the Icon*, 112. Many have discussed the theosophical influence on late nineteenth- and early twentieth-century art with Vassily Kandinsky and Kazimir Malevich as the most prevalent representatives in the Russian context. See, for example, the work of Linda Hendersen, Sixten Ringbom, Susan Compton, Roger Lipsey and Sylvia Cranston.
29 An introduction with both breadthth and depth to the theosophical influence in European culture is Olav Hammer and Michael Rothstein, eds., *Handbook of the Theosophical Current* (Leiden: Brill, 2013).
30 Antonova, "On the Problem of 'Reverse Perspective'", 464–469, 467, and Antonova, *Space, Time, and Presence in the Icon*, 113.
31 Antonova, "On the Problem of 'Reverse Perspective'", 464–469, 467.
32 Antonova, *Space, Time, and Presence in the Icon*, 128.
33 Ibid., 129.
34 Ibid., 132.
35 Fabian Heffermehl, *Bildet sett fra innsiden: Ikonoklastiske og matematiske konsepter i Florenskijs omvendte perspektiv* (Uppsala: Uppsala University, 2015), 55 n. 100.
36 Clayton Crockett, "Earth", 34.
37 Heffermehl suggests that the inverted modernist icon, exemplified by Malevich's *Black Square*, has a totalizing tendency. It has kept the elevation of the form and the material, yet lost the *acheiropoietic* sense of presence, hence it inevitably elevates its artist rather than itself. *Black Square*, Heffermehl holds, turns the idealism of suprematism into a totalizing vision instead of pointing towards the humbling mystery of its own presence. Heffermehl thus points to a problematic

aspect of the suprematist movement as a spiritual movement, one that parallels my own reason for choosing to discuss the constructivists rather than the suprematists. One aspect of Heffermehl's work—as well as the present work—that needs further elaboration concerns implicitly presenting the medieval iconography as religiously, politically and ideologically innocent. Heffermehl, *Bildet sett fra innsiden*, 116.

38 Andrew Spira, *The Avant-Garde Icon: Russian Avant-Garde Art and the Icon Painting Tradition* (Burlington: Lund Humphries, 2008), 89; Yablonskaya, *Women Artists of Russia's New Age*, 100.
39 Spira, *The Avant-Garde Icon*, 89.
40 Spira, *The Avant-Garde Icon*, 91. Sarabianov suggests that Popova's architectonics do contain an element of idealism, even utopianism, simply in being a decorative architectonics as opposed to real architecture. Sarabianov, "Painting", 133.
41 Spira, *The Avant-Garde Icon*, 91.
42 In-depth discussions on the distinction between composition and construction preceded the Obmokhu exhibition in 1921, in which several constructivists exhibited their work only two months after the formation of the group (Popova had not yet joined). Christina Lodder, "The Transition to Constructivism", in *The Great Utopia: The Russian and Soviet Avant-Garde, 1915–1932* (New York: Guggenheim Museum, 1994), 267–281, 272.
43 Matvejs wrote in Russian under the pseudonym Vladimir Markov. See Vladimir Markov, "The Principles of Creativity in the Plastic [Visual] Arts: *Faktura*", trans. Jeremy Howard, in *Vladimir Markov and Russian Primitivism: A Charter for the Avant-Garde*, eds. Jeremy Howard, Irena Buzinska, and Z. S. Strother (Farnham: Ashgate, 2015), 179–216.
44 Popova, "On a Precise Criterion…", 380.

2 Released from Eden

The Western form of Christianity is "the most anthropocentric religion the world has ever seen", Lynn White stated in 1967.[1] In Christian mythology, his reasoning continued, the loving and all-powerful God creates the world, light and darkness, heavenly bodies, the Earth with animals and plants, then Adam, and finally "as an afterthought, Eve, to keep man from being lonely".[2] It is all planned for Adam's purpose—the physical world is there to serve man, the human male. Thus, White pinpointed the roots of our ecological crisis in man's dominion over creation and he suggested that, instead, we follow the Christian example of Saint Francis with his humble and egalitarian approach to nonhuman organisms.

As we saw in the introduction, there are several weak spots in White's argument. Moreover, even if one does share the basic critique embedded in White's sweeping description of Christian mythology, should Saint Francis, the back-to-nature craftsperson, replace the dominant Man, the intelligent human designer? Is that the solution?[3] Donna Haraway would not think so, forty years ago or today. The contrast between White and Haraway in that regard encapsulates a tension still present in ecotheology debates; the tension, roughly, between morally oriented thought, on the one hand, and materially oriented thought, on the other. It highlights the question of whether the material connection between humanity and nature motivates a more functional relationship between the two, or if the fact that humanity differs from nature in its capacity for responsibility and morality is what may serve a positive development. A comparison between Elizabeth Johnson's *Ask the Beasts* (2014) and Andrew Linzey's *Why Animal Suffering Matters* (2009) illustrates the tension: the former places emphasis on the physical connection between humans and animals whereas the latter underlines also the distinction, thus motivating human responsibility on moral rather than material grounds.[4] With the early Haraway and Popova, I find this very tension handled in a constructive—and I mean that almost literally—sense, establishing a position that at once acknowledges the tension, yet is finally situated beyond it.

In "A Manifesto for Cyborgs: Science, Technology, and Socialist Feminism in the 1980s" (1985) Haraway argued it was time to realise, accept and rejoice in the fact that the myth of Eden is lost. Like White, Haraway was critical of man's dominant role in the Christian myth of creation but to her, humanity's situation in her time in history instigated another solution. She explored an approach to the world based on the way of being in the 1980s—a time when the border between the human and the machine was blurred so that humanity, in her regard, was disconnected from nature in both the Eden and the Saint Francis sense. "We are cyborgs", she stated, and cyborgs have no romantic sentiments towards nature as a lost Eden because the cyborg was never there. The cyborg does not know Eden, it knows no fall, nor any original perfection, "it is not made of mud and cannot dream of returning to dust", she argued.[5] In later interviews, Haraway explained that her cyborg manifesto was partly a reaction against the "anti-science" or "back-to-nature" programmes that she encountered in the 1980s.[6] Her aim was to face the facts of what humanity had become in her time, not because it was all good but because at that time in history the cyborg position—the technological human—was a given place, one of the actual places from which to act. She wanted to show that action and change were still possible.[7] Agency had not dissolved into a technocratic abstraction or an all-powerful market organism—the cyborg world was still material, and still open to transformation. White found in Saint Francis an opening, a role model within the Christian religion that in his regard was the starting point for addressing the ecological disaster we are now facing. Haraway, on the contrary, welcomed the fact that the technological revolution has disconnected us from our Christian origins and she appeared in that sense to take White's quest for rethinking religion one step further by letting go of the kind of romanticised human–nature relationship expressed in the Saint Francis narrative.

In this chapter we explore Haraway's renegotiation of humanity in her cyborg manifesto in relation to Popova's renegotiation of the notions of art and the artist, focusing on a question arising from the point where their contributions cross paths: What is creation and what is action if the borders between artist/creator/human and art/creation/machine do not stand? Moreover, what is theology—activist theology in particular—if the distinction between creator and creation is dissolved? What could characterise a radical theology for cyborgs, an activist theology for constructors?

We are cyborgs

In her cyborg manifesto Haraway offered what she described as "an ironic political myth faithful to feminism, socialism, and materialism"—but faithful "more as blasphemy is faithful", as in taking things seriously, ironically as in a serious play.[8] The cyborg is an image of what she described in her terminology as "a cybernetic organism, a hybrid of machine and organism, a creature of social reality as well as a creature of fiction".[9] Today many of us easily recognise—more so than in 1985—the cybernetic part of our being. That part of our identities at once technological and nonphysical, yet a bodily reality, the hybrid part that extends into the Internet, the created, constructed world of machines.[10] "We live in mythic times", Haraway argued in 1985, and her manifesto was an apology for acceptance, even embrace, but also for action on the basis of this new place for humanity.[11] The border between human and machine was blurred, she argued, and with that disruption other transgressions follow; hence her manifesto was "an argument for the pleasure in the confusion of boundaries and for responsibility in their construction".[12] She suggested we take responsibility for the social relations of science and technology and embrace the skilful task of reconstructing the boundaries of daily life "in partial connections with others, in communication with all of our parts".[13] Partly because we have no choice, and partly because of the possibilities embedded in this new way of being.

Haraway contended that in Western thinking, science and politics the distinction between organism and machine, along with several related dualist distinctions, have been important to protect and to uphold. Nature has been regarded as a resource for the production of culture (as the Other crucial to the reproduction of the Self) and the world of animals, things and machines have offered humanity the identity of dominant species: these discourses correspond to the Subject and the creator/controller, respectively. When asked years later in what sense her cyborg manifesto is a feminist manifesto, Haraway's reply differentiated *semiosis* from *semiotics* suggesting that the former, in a Foucauldian discursive understanding, is about signs in their broadest sense, "bloody and fleshly", whereas semiotics is about signs in the more abstract sense, "about the text in some kind of rarefied form".[14] Feminism is to her more about the former, the hands-on movements, the actions, more verb than noun: women's moving.[15] The text as analysed in a semiotic approach depends on a strict separation of text from matter whereas a semiosis does not. Semiosis includes the material aspects of signs, the flesh and blood, and to Haraway this is what makes her cyborg manifesto feminist: "The text is always fleshly and regularly not human, not done, not man. That was feminism then and it still is for me".[16] The cyborg is beyond gender since s/he is beyond the nature versus culture distinction presupposed in male versus female dualism, yet s/he is also beyond plain distinctions between theory and practice; the cyborg is not simply a theoretical concept but at once a mythic figure, a literary figure and a genderless bodily reality.

In her more recent work Haraway has developed the anti-dualist cyborg notion beyond the spectrum of human-versus-machine, nature-versus-culture, private-versus-public to underline our entanglement as "critters", as "holoents" or as "littermates"—terms aiming to capture the fact that we human beings are animal-material-technological organisms that do not begin with ourselves but with the web of relations from which and in which we appear. With book titles such as *The Companion Species Manifesto*, *When Species Meet, Making Kin not Population* (with Adele Clark et al.) and *Staying with the Trouble*, Haraway explores a way of being in the world that is beyond the choice between hope and despair in relation to the ecological crises.[17] A way of staying with the trouble as in embracing the fact that we as organisms are embedded in a world affected by technology, a world in which we coexist with cows, pigeons, ants, mushrooms, all affected, like ourselves, by the common web in which we are situated. Recurrently critiquing the notion that we live in the Anthropocene—as if the *anthropos* would be anything other than an in-knitted piece of yarn in a web of trouble, of life and death—Haraway has introduced instead the term *Chthulucene*. The Chthulucene is a time in which we realise our embeddedness, our situatedness, that there is no way out, neither in the past nor in the future. That no saviour will come to our rescue, that the human cannot rise above the reality-web to offer a technological escape, that the choice between hope and despair must be substituted with a truly relational existence. Or, as she states this in *Staying with the Trouble*, "recuperation is still possible, but only in multispecies alliance, across the killing divisions of nature, culture and technology and of organism, language, and machine".[18]

The later Haraway will be one of our conversation partners in Chapter 4. In the present chapter we stay primarily with the Haraway of the 1980s because I find the human–machine connection a more challenging place to begin twisting a Christian view of humanity, as opposed to the notion of the entangled organism. Going directly to the later Haraway or dragging the later Haraway straight into Christian thinking could easily evoke notions of the grand design—the ongoing mysterious creations of a first mover. For Haraway, the very notion of a singular God is inevitably linked with the tendency to distract, disconnect and disengage the human species from the life-web.[19] When thinking theology by way of Haraway, we should be careful not to mutate her thinking unduly, in ways that are at odds with her endeavour. The cyborg manifesto explicitly breaks with the Christian dream of Eden and in doing so echoes the Russian constructivist ambition to rethink the role of the creator in the creative process. It may help to wind, bend and prise ourselves away from the habitual Christian opposition between the creation and creator.

As already noted, in Haraway's terminology of the 1980s Western think-ing is characterised by dualist distinctions—nature versus culture, human versus machine—or, in her wording, "the Western traditions of racist, male-dominant capitalism".[20] To Haraway, the male-dominated Western "reli-gion"—religion here used in White's broad sense—needs an Other, and the Christian myth of creation follows this pattern. To create, to produce and to reproduce in the Christian myth of creation, presupposes dualist relations: the created needs a creator, a design needs an intelligent designer. The world is created, made to exist through a Thou affirming an I. But in the techno-logical stage of being depicted by Haraway in 1985 it is not so straightfor-ward: "It is not clear who makes and who is made in the relation between human and machine", she states.[21] Who is passive and who is active in the relationship between a human and her iPhone, who is in control? Where does the identity of the one end and the identity of the other begin? "Modern machinery", Haraway states—long before the iPhone invaded our lives—"is an irreverent upstart god, mocking the Father's ubiquity and spirituality".[22] The world of machines presents us with other nonphysical omnipresences than that of the intelligent male-designer of Christian mythology: say, for example, a social-media web, an Internet-based economy, a surveillance system and more. These other nonphysical omnipresences, these machinic ubiquities and spiritualities, challenge the very notion of creation under-stood as a dualist relation.

Machines do not have an inventor but are invented, or invent themselves, with the assistance of many who are in turn affected by machines at the very core of their being.[23] Viewing ourselves as cyborgs, machines are no longer our opposites but part of our being, if we follow Haraway; they are not the negative result of a lost Eden, not a lost creator-versus-created relation, not the effect of the fall, but just the way things are. Our notion of life and death, what kills and what doesn't, what is possible and what isn't, what a life may entail, how far we may travel, how fast we may wash our clothes, are entan-gled with our machinic way of being, dependent on machines as part of humanity. Civilisation as we know it is a washing machine, and we are part of it. Haraway proposes that we embrace this fact—again, not because it is all good but because it is where we are, it is what we have become. Even if our civilisation will change—and it will, things may take longer, we may travel more slowly, at best—it will not be a going back. "The machine is not an it to be animated, worshiped, and dominated", Haraway writes, "the machine is us, our processes, an aspect of our embodiment".[24] To embrace ourselves as machines, as cyborgs is, moreover, to open up possibilities for transgression and change in relation to each other and ourselves, as well as in relation to nature and the things that surround us. It is to stay in touch with our agency without overrating our power. For Haraway, the cyborg turns into a vision for the future as she imagines "lived social and bodily realities in which people are not afraid of their joint kinship with animals and machines, not afraid of permanently partial identities and contradictory standpoints".[25] If, on the contrary, we hold on to the illusion of a way back to the garden of Eden—a harmonic order of distinct separation yet mutual interrelation of humanity, animals and nature—we delude ourselves and potentialities for change will remain an immaterial illusion. In Haraway's view we need not a dream-like return to Saint Francis but a vision, a myth, a manifesto for cyborgs.[26]

Still, just what is change, creativity and creation in this "new" world? If no longer shaped by the duality and linearity of creator-versus-created, does not the very notion of creation change? And what is action? What is it *to create* and what, in turn, is it to *be a creator*—even the Creator?[27] In their aim to rethink art—and to rethink society along with art—the Russian constructivists accented that very question in their own characteristic way. The question of what creative activity is without the presupposed dualism of the artist as creator and art as her creation—without the dualism distinguishing reality as objective versus artistic representation as subjective—was at the heart of their revisioning of art and society. What is creativity if art lets go of intentionality, of depiction and representation; if, in short, the very notion of artistic creation is rethought? Let us invite Popova's thinking to accompany and complement Haraway's before we proceed to invite the two into a contemporary theological reflection.

From creation to construction

In a 1919 statement in the exhibition catalogue for the *Tenth State Exhibition: Nonobjective art and Suprematism*, Popova lists the characteristics of art that the exhibition aims to turn away from; these characteristics are all presented under the rubric "not painting but the depiction of reality" and under the subheading "aconstructiveness". They are "illusionism", literariness", "recognition" and "emotion". Her dense statement holds several keys to understanding the transformation of the very artistic activity that she, as part of the wider Russian non-objective movement at this stage, is after. Her vision is introduced first through that which she rejects: that is, art as depiction of reality not with the aim of constructing reality, but with the aim of either presenting an illusion of the real or, on the contrary, exactly depicting the real. That is not painting at all, she states. Aiming for recognition of the already known, or aiming to evoke emotion, are equally characteristic of what Popova disregards at this stage. Depiction, she reasons, is not painting because painting is primarily two things: "I. Architectonics." and "II. The need to transform".

Representational art that depicts and affirms reality as it is experienced by the subject—or as it *ought* to be according to inherited ideals or ideas—belongs to the past.

Instead, she describes painting as *architectonics*, an activity that aims to construct, to transform and to create the new. Not to depict or express the already experienced, not to restore long-lost ideals but to construct the yet unseen. In the three following years the theoretical framework of Popova's art develops. The exhibition for which she writes her 1919 statement is one in which suprematists, futurists and constructivists are brought together under the label of non-objectivism. Alongside her list of cons in the exhibition-catalogue statement is a list of pros, bringing together the different movements under the heading "I. Architectonics." Here, the list of pros includes: "a/ Painterly space (Cubism); b/ Line; c/ Color (Suprematism); d/ Energetics (Futurism); e/ Texture".[28] The elements with which to construct—here exemplified by space, line, colour, energetics, texture—are not new naturally, but the approach to them is. They are no longer a means for creating illusion, literary depiction, recognition and emotion but are instead tools for construction. The Russian term for "texture", *faktura*, reveals more than the English translation conveys. *Faktura* was a key concept in the Russian avantgarde and referred broadly to the constitutive materiality of the artwork. Maria Gough has depicted how the use of the term in avantgarde circles changed during the early decades of the twentieth century. In 1912, it is still primarily used to describe the working of a surface, she notes, but by 1923 *faktura* is understood as the working of the material itself; the *faktura* of the material even dictates form to the artist rather than the other way around. Hence *faktura* goes from signifying the artistic process, the working of a surface to finally signifying the site of the artistic subject's erasure, Gough concludes.[29] In a paper presented at the Institute for Artistic Culture in Moscow in 1921 Popova writes: "This is the opportune moment to create. Out of the constant old elements—old only because in the end we have only the same concrete matter—a new organization of these elements is created". The loss of origin, the leaving behind of representation opens the "old" elements to construction. The artistic movements brought together in the exhibition of 1919 differ as to *how* the elements are understood as ends: for the creation of the yet unthought, unseen and unfelt in futurism; for the demonstration of the true, inner forms of reality in suprematism and in a different sense in cubism. Yet the movement beyond art as depiction and towards an elevation of *faktura* is shared among the three movements.

Or is it? In 1922, one year after the constructivists declared their rejection of easel painting, Popova wrote a few notes to describe the works exhibited by her at the Museum for Artistic Culture, declaring that she had moved on. She described how she had gone from cubism to what she now articulated as the *organisation of the elements*.[30] Popova had been inspired by French cubist painting during her time in Paris; several works, especially of 1913, clearly show this influence. During the years 1915–1916 cubist-futurist ideas permeated her production, though the inspiration of suprematism and rayism are also notable.[31] In 1922, she explains that cubism is still dependent on a notion of representation.[32] The core of cubism, which she describes as "an analysis of the volume and space of objects", still aims to depict the objects, their volume and space; the cubist enterprise still rests on a subject analysing an object, on the depiction and representation of an absent/outer reality. The *organisation of the elements*, by contrast, aims for integral constructions—whether painted constructions of colour and plane, volume and space, or other constructions.[33] Art thus understood, she proposes, involves just as much ideological work, rethinking, as hands-on mechanical work, since it is about replacing the old criteria of an aesthetic order with new criteria of an order of construction.[34]

This was not simply about replacing the old with the new—discarding inherited forms, thoughts, expressions. Popova was explicitly indebted to the history of art, and her ideas at this stage could be said to reflect ideas in medieval iconography.[35] The intent was rather to change how the cultural and physical material with which she worked was viewed. This new order, art as construction, requires an entirely new account of creation and hence of the creator. Creation, in Popova's understanding in 1922, no longer commences with the creator but is already at work in the relation between elements. The creative process does not begin with the creator aiming to represent a thought, an idea, an experience of reality by way of a given material—through an object that she dominates—but with the encounter between the constructor and the elements of line, plane, volume, colour and matter already in internal play within the object. Popova explains: "The significance of each of these elements (line, plane, volume, colour, material) of the means of representation is made the concrete work of the given material, determining the function of the thing itself (be it utilitarian or abstract)".[36] The meaning of the very tools for representation is the work of the given material, the *faktura*. The material world has a will, and the constructor functions not as its creator but as its mechanic. Thus, materiality constitutes meaning—meaning is not an abstraction projected on the material but a construction arising from it through the encounter with the constructor and the words she uses to explain the process.

After a vocal and ballet performance at the Krivoi Dzhimmi Summer Theatre in Moscow that same year (1922), Popova wrote in frustration: "O EXPEDIENCY! If only YOU could be our criterion for a while". The performance is stuck in repressive aesthetic ideals, she states, causing it to disregard the transformative will and force of the material as well as the social world.

> Beginning with the simplest clumps of protoplasm in the organic world and ending with the most complex inventions of the human mind, all the vital factors of our world are directed toward expediency and change, according to their will—and are sometimes engendered by them.[37]

To Popova at this stage, reality stands forth as a dynamic materiality on all levels, and any artistic production that does not share her vision is a cause of nuisance for her. Wherever she looks she finds her notion of reality affirmed—and yet the artistic world at large continues in ignorance to follow old aesthetic ideals. "All life in the person of sociology, chemistry, physics, mathematics, engineering, technology, and so on advances thousands of necessities upon us, dictates us a unified and unitary approach to evaluating vital facts".[38] Everything affirms her own conviction of what art must be and do in her time, yet very few seem to see what she sees, few share her radical vision of the changes needed within the art world: "How, in the name of everything on earth and in heaven, can the most subjective and shaky of all subjective judgments, the notorious *aesthetic* judgment, serve as the criterion?"[39]

Her frustration and conviction also express, in my view, the uncompromising determination of the newly saved (to be discussed further in Chapters 3 and 4). She is impatient to abandon aesthetic ideals and to collaborate in forming a new artistic paradigm, one for which the artistic aim is functionality based on the unity of humanity, technology and nature. We may remind ourselves, however, that the most active years of Popova's artistic career—the period discussed in this book—spans roughly 1914 to 1924, a decade during which many statements were made, many collaborations in different constellations, many artistic experiments were tried, many laughs were had. The expediency of Popova's thinking is expressed even more in her readiness to change her mind—her constant experimentality—than it is in the steadfastness of her statements. In fact, it may well be her devoutness at each stage that makes her draw out the consequences of her ideas to the very end, letting them instigate an actual practice. Hence we, not without scepticism, may have to take the good along with the bad.[40]

The cyborg constructor

With Popova's constructivist approach, creative activity moves beyond the dualist subject–object relationship of the Christian myth of creation (as critically described by White and Haraway); creation becomes construction: verb/noun, active/passive, a construction that constructs. Artistic practice is not about intentionality or expressing feelings or experiences but about becoming a thing among things—an active thing, but not a dominant thing. The constructivist idea was that anyone deeply acquainted with the elements—whether physical or cultural—and having entered into them has left behind the ideas of representation, of external realities, of styles as theoretical metastructures; anyone who had truly left behind art-historical formal dogmatics and studied the elements from within could do what they did. Thus, the lost origin was not replaced by the artistic subject but by the artistic *activity* situated in the very relation between humanity, nature and technology. Or rather, beyond the distinction between them in the process and the possibility of construction.

This understanding of creativity and of the creator is pertinently expressed in an emblematic photo of Varvara Stepanova taken by her life partner Aleksandr Rodchenko in 1924.[41] Stepanova is seen up close, a cigarette in the corner of her mouth, holding a compass with which she is drawing optic silhouettes, focusing on the task alone. The activity produces a pattern without her hand touching the surface on which she is drawing. Anyone holding the compass could do what she did—or at least that is the idea. As Christina Kiaer points out, the individual creator is in focus not as a creator caught up in mystifying inspiration but as a constructor aiming for useful invention.[42] Stepanova is dependent on the instrument, on the material and together the three, the compass, the constructor and the paper—and of course the photographer, the camera, the reproduction process enabling us to view it—make out a constructing machine, replacing both the genius creator and the back-to-nature craftsperson with a mechanic, a constructor or even construction as such. In fact, the lighting makes Stepanova look like a goddess—a cigarette-smoking, curly-headed, focused god-mechanic or icon-painter perhaps, using not her fingertip to give life as in the Sistine Chapel ceiling but dependent instead on her tools and instruments, her cyborg parts and on the physicality of reality. To Popova, the artistic approach they shared reached beyond the plain technique with which to work; it was grounded in an understanding of the world in which the constructive activity—the need for transformation and expediency—were present in "the simplest clumps of protoplasm in the organic world" as well as in "the most complex inventions of the human mind".[43] Matter was to her all the elements—including light, rays, planes, volume—and as a constructor she must enter into the midst of the material, into the laboratory in order to get to know thoroughly the material, and into the factory where the distinctions between artist and art, subject and object, human and machine are transgressed through the production process.[44]

The artist, now the *constructor*, assists the elements in the ongoing process of construction while also being reconstructed in the process, simultaneously active and passive. The creative subject is replaced by what could be described as the material's assistant; thus the entire discourse surrounding and upholding the notion of the artistic subject was questioned along with the distinctions between subject and object, humanity, nature and technology.[45] Popova's constructor is therefore, I will argue, closer to the cyborg than to Adam the *anthropos* and closer to the cyborg than to God the Creator. Through the notion of the constructor, the artistic self, as Briony Fer underlines, becomes a negation—becomes "not an artist"—thus the notion of *art* and related categories, such as *male* and *female* (due to the heavily gendered notion of the creator) are destabilised along with it.[46] While the move beyond gender-dualism is not as explicit in Popova as it is in Haraway, the ambition is there also in Popova's work, as can be noticed in her clothing designs (discussed in Chapter 3).[47] The constructor challenges distinctions and ideas relating to the role of the artistic creator, even the creator's gender position, and the relationship between the creator and the created—thus finally the very notion of creation as such.

Theology constructors

In Haraway's myth, the key difference between the cyborg and the human—the difference that enables a transgression of former distinctions and ways of being—is precisely the relation to creation. What characterises the cyborg in Haraway's regard is that it has no origin, no first nature from which its culture was created. The natural state of being in the cyborg manifesto is therefore one bereft of the border between humanity and machine, and in consequence it is one without clear distinctions between nature and technology, nature and culture, or even creation and creator. Popova's notion of the constructor, while not relating to Christian mythology, rests on a similar rejection of the origin, inducing a similar reconstruction of creation as such. The constructor in Popova's regard has left behind the artistic task of representation and depiction and has substituted expediency, the need to transform and the organisation of the elements. The constructor has no origin to represent, and it is this leaving behind of the artistic paradigm of representation that opens the old inherited elements to the possibilities of construction. The task of a mechanic is not to depict reality by way of the material elements with which she works but to organise the elements into something that functions: something that works internally and externally in relation to the place, the situation and the current moment in history. The cyborg mechanic, born outside of Eden, is therefore our *theology constructor* in the current experimental endeavour.

But why? What makes the cyborg mechanic *theological*? In what sense can the constructor be understood as a theological function? Let me explain my line of thought. With Haraway and Popova we have made a move from the Creator to the constructor, from creation to the very possibility to construct. Thus, we have also moved away from a notion of the divine as a singular, nonphysical (because *meta*-physical) origin, towards a notion of divinity as the very creative possibility as such—the constructive possibility that is as present in the material world as in the abstract world of ideas. In other words, the Creator now understood as construction itself. Not a force holding a distant all-seeing synoptic vision but a potentiality haptically present in every now, seeing from within rather than from without (to invoke Heffermehl). The icon technique discussed in the previous chapter, influencing the Russian avantgarde, has brought a physical rather than theoretical theological wisdom into the constructivist artistic and political endeavour, here picked up in its avantgarde form as a theological opening for our time. A notion of a noisy (to speak with Matvejs), pluriform, hands-on divinity/creativity that sees from within the elements, thus at once scatters and unites what was formerly distinct.[48] Blurring the distinctions between matter, humanity, divinity, thus at once bringing them closer to each other and opening for other co-operations, categories and effects than those expected in the ordered notion of divided positions. A practical theological knowledge intermingling, as knowledge always does, with the other knowledges, in this case political, artistic and more.

It is a notion of radical *synergeia* in the sense of a co-working of the material world, the elements, the constructors and the constructive possibility itself. Or, possibly, a radical monergism if the gift of grace is understood as a complete reception of the gift of interdependence, as argued by Terra Schwerin Rowe.[49] The fact that we are embodied—things among things—and as such situated in time, in process and change, grounds our cyborg being, according to Haraway, to the point that the distinction between human and machine is no longer upheld in any simple sense. With no origin to long for, no paradise to mourn, the cyborg may take pleasure in its machine skill. Haraway: "Intense pleasure in skill, machine skill, ceases to be a sin, but an aspect of embodiment".[50] Similarly, the constructor having replaced the artist—the creative subject relating to the world of objects—is free to construct. Not at her own will, but in relation to the material and cultural elements of which she is a part. The notion of the theology constructor is thus based on a notion of divinity as construction itself, neither more nor less: a hope, a constant possibility, but no final solution.

In the introduction I quoted White's claim that to a Christian a tree can be no more than a physical fact. We noted that many have argued that White overlooks the sacramentality of nature in many Christian traditions; yet we countered with Crockett's argument that such Christian thinking still places the natural world second after the spiritual world.[51] We could add that the sacramentality of nature does not seem to have stopped Christians in general from cutting down trees when needed for human purposes, and in this regard White's argument still stands. If a cyborg could be a Christian, however, White's statement may be challenged so that a tree, a stone, a construction, a machine could be more than a plain physical fact; it could be a co-worker, a part of the construction that is us. We no longer live in "the Creation" but on a construction site comprising pieces, fragments, elements of past and future, material and immaterial things, machines, thoughts, images and stories. The cyborg, the theology constructor, has embraced its pluriform becoming and can approach the tree as, similarly, a pluriform haptic presence (as, possibly, Saint Francis did "off the screen" of traditional pastoral representations). We approach the tree, that is, not as a romantic idea of "the natural", not as a reminiscence of a distant moment of Creation, but as a physical mystery that demands respect and humility, just as we cyborgs do. Following Popova, we are in the present, humble towards the elements, towards the past, yet aware of the possibilities to act, to take part in construction. Thus, a theology for cyborgs would not be a return-to-nature religion, would not be about reclaiming the holy tree because God-as-nature, as lost origin to which we must return, is merely a reversal of the detached transcendent God. If we substitute God for matter/nature, immanence for transcendence, the logic of Eden understood as the logic of the first origin still stands. The cyborg/constructor is different, however, since it introduces a living-with that is without the innocent perfection of Eden, yet with responsibility, humility and the possibility to act. Divinity as construction. The notion of divinity as construction closely relates to process theology, including concepts such as Catherine Keller's notion of the *tehom* as the deep of constant becoming out of which the world was created.[52] Yet precisely in its aim *not* to ground theology in its creational moment, its origin, the notion of divinity as construction is instead an experiment with a God-notion that is less dependent on historical linearity. It thus challenges the theological custom of historical legitimisation.

A theology for constructors is for all who see the material world as our dwelling place, the material world as it appears to us: a merging of ideas and things, of past and future in the present; a world not imagined as more perfect elsewhere, before the fall, or after redemption—or it could be imagined that way, but just as a couple of ideas among many. A radical theology for constructors is not detached from the environment but incarnated in it, not fleeing to a mythic garden, nor to a lost ideal relation to "mother nature", but starting from where we stand, as we are, that rectangular extension of our hand included.

Notes

1 Lynn White, "The Historical Roots of Our Ecological Crisis", 1205.
2 Ibid.
3 For an overview as well as a profound discussion of criticism of the White thesis, see Espeth Whitney, "Lynn White Jr.'s 'The Historical Roots of Our Ecological Crisis' After 50 Years", *Wiley Online Library*, 28 August 2015, https://doi.org /10.1111/hic3.12254.
4 See Sofia Proofh, *Gläd er och jubla ständigt över det som jag skapar: En jäm-förande textanalys om djurrätt och miljöpåverkan ur ett teologiskt perspektiv*, kandidat-uppsats, Stockholm School of Theology, 2018.
5 Donna Haraway, "A Manifesto for Cyborgs: Science, Technology, and Socialist Feminism in the 1980s", in *Feminism/Postmodernism*, ed. Linda J. Nicholson (New York: Routledge, 1990), 191–233, 192.
6 Donna Haraway, in an interview by Nicholas Gane, "When We Have Never Been Human, What is to Be Done? Interview with Donna Haraway", *Theory, Culture and Society* 23, no. 7–8 (2006): 135–158, quote on 156.
7 Cyborg is here broadly understood as a human dependent upon technology. For a fascinating discussion on theology in relation to different posthuman notions see Scott Midson, *Cyborg Theology: Humans, Technology and God* (London: I.B. Tauris, 2017).
8 Haraway, "A Manifesto for Cyborgs", 190.
9 Haraway, "A Manifesto for Cyborgs", 191.
10 The field of theology and technology is now established with titles such as Brad J. Kallenberg, *God and Gadgets: Following Jesus in a Technological Age* (Oregon: Cascade, 2011) and Celia-Deane Drummond, Sigurd Bergmann, and Bronislaw Szerszynski, *Technofutures, Nature and the Sacred* (Farnham: Ashgate, 2015), and a research network on techno-theology based at Stockholm School of Theology, Sweden.
11 Her later work suggests the ideas presented here are still pivotal, though developed especially regarding the environmental consciousness. See, for instance, *Staying with the Trouble: Making Kin in the Cthulucene* (Durham: Duke University Press, 2016).
12 Haraway, "A Manifesto for Cyborgs", 191.
13 Haraway, "A Manifesto for Cyborgs", 223.
14 Gane, "When We Have Never Been Human", 135–158, 137.
15 Gane, "When We Have Never Been Human", 136.
16 Gane, "When We Have Never Been Human", 137.
17 Donna Haraway, *The Companion Species Manifesto: Dogs, People, and Significant Others* (Chicago: University of Chicago Press, 2003); *When Species Meet* (Minneapolis: University of Minnesota Press, 2007); *Making Kin Not Population: Reconceiving Generations* (Chicago: Prickly Paradigm, 2018); *Staying with the Trouble: Making Kin in the Chthulucene* (Durham: Duke University Press, 2016).
18 Donna Haraway, *Staying with the Trouble*, 118.
19 For an example that supports my point and is an excellent theological contribution, see Midson's discussion on the Chthulucene potential of Genesis. Scott

Midson, "Humus and Sky Gods: Partnership and Post/Humans in Genesis 2 and the Chthulucene," *Sofia* (2018), https://doi.org/10.1007/s11841-018 -0664-7.

20 Haraway, "A Manifesto for Cyborgs", 191.
21 Haraway, "A Manifesto for Cyborgs", 219.
22 Haraway, "A Manifesto for Cyborgs", 195.
23 Who is the creator of open-source computer systems where anyone with enough skill may contribute to the product, a product without end but existing through a continuous chain of updates?
24 Haraway, "A Manifesto for Cyborgs", 222.
25 Haraway, "A Manifesto for Cyborgs", 196.
26 Haraway, "A Manifesto for Cyborgs", 196.
27 The later Haraway denounces those words—creation, creator, creatures— because of the dualism they entail. She uses, instead the word "critters" precisely because the "taint of 'creatures' and 'creation' does not stick to 'critters'" and she adds, "if you see such a semiotic barnacle, scrape it off". Critters, to her, "refers promiscuously to microbes, plants, animals, humans and nonhumans, and sometimes even to machines". Haraway, *Staying with the Trouble*, 169.
28 Liubov Popova, "Statement from the Catalog for the 'Tenth State Exhibition: Nonobjective Art and Suprematism'", in *Liubov Popova*, eds. Dimitri V. Sarabianov and Natalia L. Adaskina, trans. Marian Schwartz (New York: Harry N. Abrams, 1990), 346–347, 347.
29 Maria Gough, "Faktura: The Making of the Russian Avant-Garde", *Res 36* (Autumn 1999): 32–59, 32.
30 Liubov Popova, "For the Museum of Artistic Culture", in *Liubov Popova*, eds. Dimitri V. Sarabianov and Natalia L. Adaskina, trans. Marian Schwartz (New York: Harry N. Abrams, 1990), 359.
31 Sarabianov, "Painting", 57.
32 Sarabianov notes how cubism "seemingly frees itself from the direct movement toward nature, granting the artist freedom to interpret the world of objects". In the end, however, the cubist face was rather "the final stage in a more or less continuous contact with reality". Sarabianov, "Painting", 59.
33 Popova, "For the Museum of Artistic Culture", 359.
34 Popova, "For the Museum of Artistic Culture", 359.
35 See the reasoning on Heffermhel in Chapter 1.
36 Popova, "For the Museum of Artistic Culture", 359.
37 Liubov Popova, "On a Precise Criterion", 380.
38 Popova, "On a Precise Criterion", 380.
39 Popova, "On a Precise Criterion", 380.
40 Tom Sandqvist even suggests Popova was overly eager to take to new trends and hence suggests it is not unlikely that she would have adopted to the demands of the Stalinistic regime had she lived to experience them. Sandqvist, *Det andra könet i öst*, 115.
41 Printed in Christina Kiaer, *Imagine no Possessions: The Socialist Objects of Russian Constructivism* (Cambridge: MIT, 2005), 99.
42 Kiaer, *Imagine no Possessions*, 100.
43 Popova, "On a Precise Criterion", 380.
44 V. F. Stepanova and L. S. Popova, "Memo to the Directorate for the First State Cotton-Printing Factory", unpublished manuscript, 1924, Rodchenko-Stepanova Archive, Moscow, cited in Kiaer, *Imagine no Possessions*, 94.
45 Gough, "Faktura", 52

46 Briony Fer, "What's in a Line? Gender and Modernity", *The Oxford Journal of Modern Art* 13, no. 1 (1990): 77–88, 87.

47 The following quote from a reflection over the costume making for the legendary production of *The Magnanimous Cuckold* in 1922 is telling: "In all, the costume was intended for seven or eight sorts or types of work. There was a fundamental disinclination to making any distinction between the men's and women's costumes; it just came down to changing the pants to a skirt or culottes". Liubov Popova, "Introduction to the Inkhuk Discussion of *The Magnanimous Cuckold*", in *Liubov Popova*, eds. Dimitri V. Sarabianov and Natalia L. Adaskina (New York: Harry N. Abrams, 1990), 378–379.

48 See discussion on Matvejs and iconography in Chapter 1.

49 People of faith are taught to trust, Rowe notes, rather than fear the fact that we are linked to something bigger, that we "belong body and soul to a larger story", a story in which we are also responsible. Terra Schwerin Rowe, *Toward a Better Worldliness: Ecology, Economy, and the Protestant Tradition* (Minneapolis: Fortress, 2017), xii.

50 Haraway, "A Manifesto for Cyborgs", 222.

51 Andreas Nordlander points out the many Christian sources that point precisely to the sacrality of the trees and hence to the weakness of White's argument. As stated, we need every ecotheological voice at this stage, hence I encourage those who are provoked by White's article to engage with the excellent work of Nordlander and others. Those who, on the contrary, are sympathetic towards White's critique may find a theological opening in the radical theology tradition. See e.g. Andreas Nordlander, "Green Purpose, Teleology, Ecological Ethics, and the Recovery of Contemplation", *Studies in Christian Ethics*, first published online: March 4, 2020, https://doi.org/10.1177%2F0953946820910672.

52 Catherine Keller, *Face of the Deep: A Theology of Becoming* (New York: Routledge, 2003), xvi.

3   The things you own

Paul Tillich famously criticised Salvador Dali's *The Sacrament of the Last Supper* (1955), declaring that the painting was "Simply junk!"—to which Dali responded: "I have been drinking mineral water exclusively for more than ten years!" Dali's answer is not as bizarre as it might seem. Dali misheard Tillich, thinking he had said "Simply drunk!" But setting the humour aside, Tillich's strong reaction is indicative of his notion of the theological aspect of art. Dali may have used a Christian *form* in his playful interpretation of the last supper, but the *meaning*, the religious style, Tillich reasoned, shared nothing of the style or meaningfulness of theological expressions of the very ground of being. Dali's work rather approached "religious kitsch" which, to Tillich, merely masks the absence of religious style with empty religious *Inhalt*.[1] The sacredness of art for Tillich had to do with the *Gehalt* of the work—the religious meaning—not with the religious content, *Inhalt*, itself. Or as Tillich tellingly puts it elsewhere, "it is not an exaggeration to ascribe more of the quality of sacredness to a still-life by Cézanne or a tree by van Gogh than to a picture of Jesus by Uhde".[2]

Thinking of the complexity of the human relationship to things, though, of the many prayers, tears, hopes and dreams expressed in front of religious kitsch (low-quality icons hanging from rear-view mirrors in taxis, pastel Christ images folded in wallets, or held by sweaty hands in times of fear or sorrow)—thinking in other words of objects in general and objects of religious art in particular, is there not an oversimplification in Tillich's judgement of authentic religious style versus religious kitsch? Does not the very complexity of the human relationship to things—art objects included—deserve a humbler theological reflection? Because if we are to rethink religion broadly speaking in relation to the material world as suggested by White, is not a good place to start our relationship to the things of our everyday life, to the things we own and how we relate to them?

In the present chapter we explore what I have described as a merger of the spiritual and the political in Popova. By comparing Popova to Vladimir

Tatlin, we shall discover a point of convergence between Popova and Walter Benjamin. Both Popova and Benjamin take the spiritual into regard when thinking material reality, thus making room for an ambiguity in our habitual understanding of the distinction between the material versus the spiritual. Hence, the junction where the two meet opens a spiritual path between, or beyond, materialism and idealism. Through Popova and Benjamin, we reach beyond the choice between regarding material reality as passive and fetishised, or on the contrary as an active political force at Man's service. For both, the material world is more than a mere given, more than a first nature, but also more than what may be captured by plain human reason, thus more than a means for a human political vision. Finally, we shall return to Tillich's notion of religious style, religious *Gehalt*, and explore the notion of a *second theology*. But let us begin with a Russian debate on the material versus the spiritual.

A new everyday

The distinction between public and private in Russian political thought differs, broadly speaking, from that of Western models. The major cultural opposition in Russia is not between private and public existence but between material and spiritual existence, between *byt* and *bytie*.[3] Comparing the "American dream" to the Russian dream (according to the philosophers of *The Russian Idea*), the former is more a dream of the private pursuit of happiness in the family home, whereas the latter consists of ideals such as heroic spiritual homelessness and messianic nomadism. Or, in Svetlana Boym's words: "Unpractical daydreaming is not a part of the American myth of individual self-sufficiency. Privacy, on the other hand, is not important for the 'Russian personality'".[4] The Russian notion of the material, *byt*, is connected to the repetitious, dull and heavy chores of the private everyday, which is why for the pre-revolution political thinkers in Russia *byt* was habitually understood as the reactive, unchanging aspects of life that held the revolution back. *Bytie*, by contrast—spiritual existence—was connected with the public, with change, invention, progress but also with the emotional and the transcendent. Thus, *bytie* encompassed at once the possibility for change *and* the earlier impeding paradigms of thought, including Christian transcendence, the church and longstanding societal ideals. In consequence, the overcoming of the opposition between the material (private, *byt*) and the spiritual (public, *bytie*) was an explicit goal for pre-revolution political thinkers in Russia; hence the campaign of the *novyi byt*, a new everyday life under socialism, was at the heart of the political renewal project. It was an attempt at elevating *byt*, letting the new spiritual enlightenment (spiritual in an ideological rather than a religious sense) take place on the level of the material and in the private spheres of the everyday. The campaign of the new everyday spurred intricate debates among Russian intellectuals, which will not be abundantly analysed here, but Popova's contribution must be viewed in light of the wider discourse aiming to rethink the notion of the material in relation to everyday life and the potentialities of change.

Artist Vladimir Tatlin did not describe himself as a constructivist. He underlined his independence from art movements and described his work using terms like "material culture"—but he is nonetheless often named as the movement's founder.[5] Tatlin explicitly took part in the project of transforming the everyday, *novyi byt*, as material and as social-material reality, "calling maximum attention to the simplest things that surround us".[6] He turned away from capitalist desires, suggesting we should distrust the eye and elevate touch. In other words, we should place optical vision under the control of the haptic, of touch.[7] Consequentially, he stopped creating for the galleries and began inventing instead for the home: stoves, clothing and pottery. Despite harsh words from critics deriding his new interest in "womanly matters" he persisted in his project of turning *byt* into *comrade*.[8] Tatlin's shift from high-status art to household items was a conscious invention of an active material object through which the modernist principle of "truth to materials"—the will of the medium or the material itself determining artistic form—takes on social agency.[9] If possessions and commodity in capitalism were regarded along the lines of Marxist commodity fetishism, in Tatlin's vision the fetish would instead turn into comrade. In other words, things would not be admired for *what they are* (while hiding the reality of production) but would be active and valued for *what they can do*.

Popova moves in a similar realm of thought but takes the renegotiation of the very notion of matter one step further. In papers she presented in 1921 at two art institutes in Moscow, the Inkhuk and Vkhutemas, a far-reaching renewal of the notion of the material takes place. The artistry of today, she reasoned, amounts to a transformation of the understanding of elements: a transformation of the understanding of what makes up the thing as thing— the volume, the colour, the lines, the weight.[10] The constructive possibilities of the elements may thus stand forth beyond ideas limited by habitual thinking, by notions of origin and truth, or by earlier styles or artistic ideals. Art, she wrote, is moving towards the construction of concepts rather than the depiction of concepts. Art is moving towards the organisation of the concept, hence the organisation of the thing because, she reasons, if we are to see the possibilities of this world, we must liberate the elements from representational thought.[11] For Popova, art is political because the political is material, it is concrete—colours, lines, rulers, compasses and constructions for everyday life.

Tatlin aimed explicitly to renew the notion of the material, entering into the process of the *novyi byt* by elevating functionality over beauty, touch over eye. His aim was not a plain rationality as detectable in later functionalism but rather what Maria Gough defines as "materiological determination". According to Gough, Tatlin sought to foster the volition of the material rather than to express his individual artistic will, reconfiguring himself as the material's assistant.[12] To that extent, his approach to materiality resembles that of Popova. Both aim to let the material, its inherent possibilities, aspects and levels, affect the constructions produced, and both aim to step back as artists assisting rather than controlling the material. There is, however, a difference between the two—a difference we shall delineate by way of Walter Benjamin.

Art, ritual and second technology

Walter Benjamin, inspired by the constructivist movement in Germany, approaches art history in a way that resembles that of the Russian constructivists. To Benjamin, art in the age of mechanical reproduction has lost its basis in the original; art is no longer grounded in the notion of authenticity but in action and in effect, or to borrow Benjamin's words, in being *political*. Art *is* what it *does*, what it creates and constructs. Thus Benjamin, though later than Popova, like her moves beyond the logic of representation and into the logic of performance and construction. In "The Work of Art in the Age of Mechanical Reproduction", Benjamin famously traces art back to its origin in ritual. The earliest art works, he writes, "originated in the service of a ritual—first the magical, then the religious kind".[13] The very notion of authenticity in art stems from this religious beginning in which the particular artwork—say the statue of a goddess or god—was the presence without which the ritual would lack meaning: a copy would not do. The early magical or religious function was later replaced by what Benjamin calls "the secular cult of beauty", praising the original artwork by the original artist—an analogous notion of authenticity, now in new clothing. A copy would still not do. Then came the revolution of technical reproduction, however, and suddenly art could be anywhere: could be copied, carried in a pocket, printed on demand. Photography appeared, and what was authenticity in the art of photography? "At the time", Benjamin states, "art reacted with the doctrine of *l'art pour l'art*, that is, with a theology of art".[14] The art world reacted by proclaiming art an end in itself. Art, in other words, made itself holy, an apophatic enigma not to be scrutinised; hence, art once again took on the role of the fetish, veiling its material construction and historicity.

Art for art's sake was just a phase however, Benjamin continues, before art became what it inevitably had to become after the loss of origin:

political, performative, constructive. Art became political but in different manners, Benjamin observes, and he characterises two distinctive and
even opposite expressions: *aesthetical politics* (the fascist expression)
versus *political aesthetics* (the communist expression). The former, he
argues, uses aesthetics to render the status quo attractive, to make misuse
of power beautiful and to romanticise poverty and hard work, whereas
the latter, by contrast, makes art political, using it to change the world,
to create a better society. The two aspects of political art relate, in turn,
to another of Benjamin's conceptual couples (introduced in the second
version of the essay): first versus second technology. *First technology*, in
Benjamin's sense, aims to master the world, is used to control nature and
humanity for the good of man. It is technology functioning as art did in
its early ritual stage. *Second technology*, on the other hand, aims at the
relation, the interplay between nature and humanity, and correlates to the
role of art in the age of mechanical reproduction. Second technology, in
Benjamin's use of the term, opens a possibility to make constructive use
of the loss of foundation, of the technological gap between humanity and
nature because, as Benjamin points out, the results of first technology
are eternal, whereas those of second technology are temporary.[15] Second
technology originates in play, Benjamin states, not in nature understood
as a first nature.

This conceptual couple developed out of the Hegelian notions of first
versus second nature, which Benjamin—like Georg Lukacs and Theodor
Adorno—used to call attention to the illusion of givenness: the illusion of
what is regarded as first nature. Benjamin wanted to emphasise the fact
that nature as humanly understood always instigates a relation, a technology in one form or another, and so he complicated the conceptual couple.[16]
Influenced in part by a conversation with actress and theatre director Asja
Lacis and by science-fiction writer Paul Sheerbart, Benjamin thus introduced the notions of first versus second technology in the second version of
the "Work of Art" essay. Interestingly for the purposes of this book, technology understood as a second technology focuses not on a romanticised
lost Eden in which man and nature are one, nor on human dominance of the
forces of nature which could eventuate out of a subsequent separation of
the two, but on a *functional relation* between humanity and nature as themselves operational.[17] Humanity and nature are not seen as entities, as objects
for technology, but technology is understood more like a verb at work in
the very relationality that makes both humanity and nature appear. Which
is why, in consequence, humanity and nature in such an account become
themselves operational concepts rather than active versus passive objects.

Benjamin's reasoning in the "Work of Art" essay resonates with the
theoretical foundation for Popova's artistry: the loss of an origin to

represent coheres with the political-artistic imperative ("EXPEDIENCY") of material construction resulting from that loss. In Popova's vision, art has embraced the loss of ritual as well as the loss of illusive authenticity, and has taken the possibility of technological reproduction as its starting point, artistically and practically. Having left behind the representational imperative, art is free to construct or, in the words of Benjamin, art is free to be political. The artist, for Popova, is "not an artist" but a constructor: a constructor of concepts and elements and to that extent, as artist, is also replaceable. The apophatic expression—"not an artist"—derives not from a theological analysis but from Briony Fer's art-theoretical and feminist discussion of Popova's use of lines. Yet the apophatic connotations of the expression concur with Fer's point, as with the constructivist attempt to move away from the notion of the artist as creative subject relating to a passive object. The "not" corresponds to the intention of replacing nouns with verbs in the creative processes which, in turn, corresponds to a similar move within apophatic and feminist theology.[18] It is not the artist, the individual creative mind that creates, but the function, the constructor—whoever she is—at work in relation to the material.[19] Anyone having studied and become deeply acquainted with the elements could fill the constructor function, because it was all about being free to approach the elements as elements rather than merely in accordance with artistic ideals, norms or prevalent styles. To the constructivists, the lost origin was not substituted by the artistic subject but by the artistic *activity*, which was situated in the very relation between humanity and nature—in the process of construction and the possibility of construction.

Popova's particular contribution to constructivism was known for its ambiguity. While consciously moving from the spiritual realm of suprematism into the political realm of constructivism, Popova appeared to retain an indecisiveness in her artistic approach—or rather, in my view, she indicated a third way, to be addressed now.

Beyond comrade and fetish

From 1920 onwards, Popova left the vocabulary of the spiritually oriented suprematist movement for that of the politically oriented constructivist movement, but her notion of matter was not a simple choice between art as ritual centrepiece and the art of technological reproduction as described by Benjamin. Rather, in Popova there appears to be an attempt to move beyond the dualism of the active "comrade" versus the passive, admired "fetish"— beyond the political-versus-magical, the material-versus-spiritual.

In her early painterly architectonics period, her treatment of space and planarity, colour and layering, resembled that of the Russian icon, which

Figure 3.1 Spatial Force Construction (1920)

remained a source of inspiration for her.[20] In her late paintings labelled *Spatial Force Constructions*, the spiritual dimension was still present. In what has been named her "rayic" work, she used rays to materialise—to turn into building material—the cosmic infinity earlier treated by Kazimir Malevich, Natalia Goncharova and Mikhail Larinov in explicitly spiritual terms.[21]

Unlike in Malevich's suprematism and Larinov's and Goncharova's rayism, however, Popova did not aim to capture an ideal truth of reality. The rayist movement was grounded in a certain metaphysics, in an idea of the radiant inner structure of reality. Malevich's suprematism, in turn, was (like Vassily Kandinsky's notion of the spiritual in art) grounded in an idea of the true forms of reality. Popova, on the contrary, did not aim to *achieve* reality but to *construct* reality in accordance with the constructivists' slogan:

"Life-building, not life-knowing". Still, for Popova the material with which to build life was not stable and lifeless, nor merely hands-on living, changeable matter. Her building material could just as well be rays, light, and when treating planes in her painted constructions, the planes appeared to affect each other by their very proximity. For example, in *Painterly Architectonics with a Pink Semicircle* (1918), a red plane shades into orange when approaching an orange plane, and a blue plane and a pink semicircle shine through a seemingly solid black surface. In her later *Spatial Force Construction* series of 1921, the planes relate to each other in a way that resembles at once the effect of intermingling rays of light and of solid material somehow turning fluid when colliding. Or even, as in the early cubist-futurist *Portrait of a Philosopher* (1915), she lets the figure (in this case her own brother) merge with the surrounding objects. The backdrop turns to surface, an uneven surface mixing, fusing letters with objects, background with foreground, human with matter.[22] Does that indicate a unity of diversity, as argued by Spira above? The compositions or constructions do make out a whole as they stand; but no, to me Popova's work is not aiming towards expressing unity, expressing the One, as Spira indicates. Expediency is for her as present in the material world itself as it is a constructivist artistic ideal.[23] The material world is not simply there for humanity to dominate, to make useful for human purposes, not even if the purpose is to offer the material a role of "comrade" in a human political vision. Nor, on the other hand, can the material world be placed within a human idea of the one origin, and thus be offered the role of "fetish", as when nature is regarded as culture's Other. Her artwork indicates otherwise because, when one material body encounters another, their solid identities turn fluid.

Benjamin shares with Popova this sense of complexity bordering on mystery that the human–material relation manifests. Although the notion of fetishisation surfaces in Benjamin's description of the origins of art discussed above—the ritualistic origin, the recurrent attempts at hiding its situatedness and material contingency—his own notion of *commodity as phantasmagoria* has more complex connotations. It takes seriously the fact that objects, in the borderland of humanity and nature, are more intricate than irrational, blinding fetishes.[24]

Commodity as phantasmagoria

The phantasmagoria—the *camera obscura* theatre shows—were immensely popular in many European countries in the nineteenth century. The camera obscura projected imagery of what the audience feared—as if it were there, present in the room. The audience was thrilled, scared and fascinated, enchanted, not because they thought it was real, they knew it was not, but its faux realism induced shock and emotion. Christine Blaettler argues that the notion of the phantasmagoria is a profane phenomenon—thus a critical alternative to the fetish—nuancing the notion of materiality and objects. Even in the age of technical reproduction, things seem to have a life of their own, Blaettler holds; they enchant, fascinate, frighten and enthral, hence the nuances of the phantasmagoria render possible a deeper understanding of the function of the commodity in a capitalist society. We buy things knowing they will not give us the happiness they promise. We even know the production processes often take part in degrading the environment while also heavily exploiting the workers who produce them. But still the magic of the camera obscura, the phantasmagoria, does not take one back to the ritual presence, the fetish, the pre-enlightenment god-statue, because the modern human–object relationship is more intricate. Desire, enchantment and fascination cannot be eliminated by reason.

The notion of the fetish, in both its critical and affirmative versions, depicts subjects and social collectives as passive and powerless admirers, whereas the notion of the phantasmagoria by contrast renders subjects visible by evoking the complexity of their reason and consumer responsibility. The technology of phantasmagoria finally places objects and human–object-relations within the confines of this world as constructions with an inner-worldly genealogy and material reality. In other words, the technology of phantasmagoria is beyond magic but nonetheless offers a challenge to reason. As an expression of a profane paradigm, the phantasmagoria illuminates the specifically modern—rather than modern versus premodern—tension between enchantment and disenchantment, between irrationality and the rational. The phantasmagoria thus links sensual perception, irrationality, artistic imagination, technological production and critical reflection.[25] Let us therefore bring the notion of the commodity as phantasmagoria into the delineation of the difference between Popova and Tatlin in order to let Benjamin's concepts illuminate the point of convergence as well as the point of divergence. In their aim to rethink the material, to rethink the distinction between *byt* and *bytie*, Tatlin and Popova both aim for an art that is political in Benjamin's sense of the word. Both aim, moreover, for an art of the second technology—art that is not used to master the world but rather to handle the relation between humanity and matter. I will argue, though, that the difference between the two figures stands forth at the level of what Benjamin terms the phantasmagoria.

Tatlin's vision of the artist becoming the material's assistant, thus turning *byt* into comrade, making dead matter into social agent, does elevate the material as such; but in doing so, I suspect that it elevates human reason along with a romantic-utopian notion of nature.[26] Tatlin's vision is not about controlling nature—it does not seek a return to Eden in White's sense—yet it is about controlling the mind to achieve a natural yet utopian relation to the material world. If only we were to see more clearly, Tatlin seems to argue, we would gain the requisite maturity to handle the material world in a more natural and constructive way. Human sensibility lifting itself above the fetishised notion of nature into a more natural state, in Tatlin's vision, offers the political and artistic solution.[27] To that extent his vision still appears to rest on an account of reality in which human domination is presupposed,

Figure 3.2 Textile design (1924)

and in which humanity "rises above" the lure of the phantasmagoria. He understands what has to be overcome in the human account of objects more in terms of the fetish than in terms of the phantasmagoria. The failure of Tatlin's "Street Dress" is an illustrative example.[28] It was a cotton dress

Figure 3.3 Design for a dress (1924)

designed for mass production. The fabric was affordable, durable, easy to wash, easy to dry and the model was designed for cheap production, for mobility, comfort and freedom of movement. It was, in short, Tatlin's vision of the new everyday in one dress. Yet unsurprisingly, the original prototype of the dress was the only one ever made. In the singular photograph of it—in which Tatlin himself wears it—Google it and take a look; would you ever desire to wear such a dress? Tatlin's high confidence in human reason, his faith in the idea that the fetish-awe could be overcome by sensibility and by an appeal to the natural, made him disregard the complexity of the human relation to the material world, and thus overlook the modern complex of enchantment versus disenchantment, of irrational desire versus critical thinking in relation to the things we own. In other words, he disregarded the phantasmagoric aspect of commodity.

When Popova made a similar move away from the galleries and towards fabric and clothing design, her approach was another. If Tatlin risked moving into a historically female area of design, Popova risked her entire status as a respected artist for the same transition. She designed textile fabrics that, unlike Tatlin's, were in fact mass produced, affordable and practical, with optic, nonobjective patterns.[29]

The patterns were to point towards the production process, hence to strengthen the ideal of transparency of construction, while also being at least in theory possible to fabricate without an artist's hand touching the material. Popova designed dresses in accord with these ideals, with an express aim to appeal to women's desire, while simultaneously offering alternative expressions of femininity. Unlike Tatlin's designs, which were oriented towards hygiene and warmth, Popova's dresses set up a deliberate confrontation between what Kiaer describes as "the rational product of socialist industry and the commodity fetish".[30] With her flapper dress, for example, Popova aimed to create a dress that women would desire yet would be affordable, and would allow women to move freely and give them a sense of beauty that was not an objectified or sexualised beauty.[31]

Whether she succeeded or not is up to the wearers to decide, but the attempt as such indicates that Popova's outlook comes closer to Benjamin's complex account of commodity as phantasmagoria than to Tatlin's trust in consumer sensibility. After Popova's death in 1924, an issue of *Lef* was dedicated to her legacy; in it the editors' description of her late fabric-design work is telling: "Popova was a Constructivist-Productivist not only in words, but in deed (…) attempting, in one creative act to unite the demands of economics, the laws of exterior design and the mysterious taste of the peasant woman from Tula".[32] In a famous quote, Popova says she has never been as happy as when a peasant woman freely chose a fabric designed by her for her dress.[33] Considering the intricacy of her artistic aim, there is reason to believe she actually meant what she said. Desire is enigmatic, which is why design must meet consumers as the mysteriously desiring creatures they are, even when the designers' goal is to free consumers from being fetishisers of the things they own. Tatlin trusted in reason to discern the volition of the material that leads to a good and comfortable life. Individual enlightenment in relation to matter would lead the way to a new everyday life—not to control matter, as in the idea of a first technology, but still to control humanity through reason in its relation to matter. Popova, by contrast, acknowledged the complexity of the human–nature relation, and recognised that it was beyond the reach of reason, an intricate web of material-symbolic connections.

Second theology

Human reason is not sensible but driven by opaque desires, by an expediency that the human mind cannot fully understand or fathom, much less control, which is why humility is needed in relation to the physical as well as the nonphysical world. The possibility of construction, in consequence, is an enigma of infinite mechanical options, and reality is a construction site limited only by the physical and nonphysical material at hand. By introducing these ideas into a theological discussion and applying them in the very practice of academic theology, can we approach what one may speak of as a *second theology*? Can we approach a theological practice that has taken construction as its very foundation? Not that it has never been done before—theologies of ongoing creation reach far back in the history of theology—but because concepts, new constellations of ideas, create new perceptions of reality, they take part in the very construction of theology, here in relation precisely to the loss of foundation in the technological, environmental and theological reality of our time.

In parallel with Benjamin's notion of first versus second technology—deriving from the first versus second nature—a *first theology* would be a theology that in one way or another understands an Eden as its origin, which is why it seeks eternal answers and solutions by turning back. *Second theology*, on the contrary, would be a theology grounded in play, released from Eden, not striving for access to any origin, not believing in humanity's ability to dominate nature, not even believing in the distinction between nature and culture as such, since it would be a theology for which nouns would be verbs, functions operating in relation. From the point of view of second theology, there would be no untouched or innocent aspects of reality. A second theology would acknowledge that theology is for mechanics of ongoing construction—not for archaeologists uncovering a truth deeply hidden away. A second theology would recognise its task not as pertaining to Christian truth tout court but to *the relationship between humanity and the idea of Christian truths*. Thus, it would be a truly *political* theology in

Benjamin's sense of the word. Just as art turns political when it has realised its loss of the original and become function rather than depiction, in Benjamin's reasoning, so a second theology would be a political theology—a theology that *does*, a theology that *acts*. A second theology would not believe that clear thinking can free the mind from dreams and desires, not even from longing for an Eden that never was. Our relationship to reality is too intricate, too enigmatic. Religious kitsch, for instance—does it not resemble the phantasmagoric theatre shows? We may not believe that Jesus, the son of God, is actually present in a picture by Uhde, but even so—when fear strikes we fold our fingers around the image *as if he is*.

A second theology would not accept Tillich's distinction between religious kitsch and religious *Gehalt* or meaning. A second theology would argue that religious meaning is constructed in the in-between of humanity and Christian ideas and artefacts; if reality is a construction site, meaning is mysterious not because it is eternal and immaterial but because it is contingent and material. Materiality constitutes meaning. Meaning is not an abstraction assigned to material reality but a construction arising from matter through the encounter with the consumer or mechanic and the words and ideas she uses to explain what happens. Religious *Gehalt*, religious style or meaning, is not there for anyone to discover but appears as a function on the surface through the encounter with bodies, dreams, fears and desires. Benjamin's notion of commodity as phantasmagoria instigates a certain humility in relation to religious artefacts—whether images created by artists like da Vinci, Uhde or Dali, or chalices, or bread and wine. We know the bread and wine are not flesh and blood, but neither are they just bread and wine. Matter is more than reason may capture, but also more than what is suggested by the very distinction between the spiritual and the material.

Second theology is neither immanent nor transcendent, neither purely secular nor purely sacred; it can be all of these because it approaches theology at the level of appearance, at the surface of appearances, which is at once an inherent mystery and a plain fact. As Benjamin explains the playful force of the second technology:

> Just as a child who has learned to grasp stretches out its hand for the moon as it would for a ball, so humanity, in its effort for innervation, sets its sights as much on currently utopian goals as on goals within reach.[34]

The distinction between first and second theology would not relate to where the divine is situated—in or beyond this world—but how the theological task is understood, which in turn affects how theological knowledge is regarded. To second theology, theological knowledge is constantly constructed, materially, with or without us—not something we discover. If it is historical, it is so in the present. Recalling Buber's question—"Theology, how do you do that?"—we could suggest second theology as a form of activism, politically, ecologically, socially and academically. Not to throw out the old traditions and prompt a new utopian order, but to critique and reconstruct with the conviction that the mystery of the material world always surpasses what we think we know. Second theology could be performed on the streets, in the trees, on the seas, in churches and town halls—expedient and playful.

A second-theology construction as a piece of writing, as academic theology, what would that look like? Second *technology*, in the words of Daniel Mourenza, "is based on testing and scientific procedures, that is, on experimentation and play (*Spiel*)".[35] In other words, it parallels Haraway's cyborg approach and is in that sense an approach to nature after humanity's release from Eden, after the dream of the idyllic origin has evaporated.[36] Playful, experimental, never claiming the last word but rather always adding yet another. Similarly, a second *theology* for cyborgs could be one that, following Haraway, refuses to demonise technology and precludes an anti-science metaphysics, and does so because the living-with today is inescapably a cyborg living-together. In the next chapter, we endeavour to create such a second-theology construction.

Notes

1 Re Manning, "Tillich's Theology of Art", 158.
2 Paul Tillich, *The Religious Situation* (2003); file:///D:/rb/relsearchd.dll-action =showitem&gotochapter=3&id=18.htm (2 of 7) [2/4/03 1:42:14 PM], accessed 1 June 2018.
3 Svetlana Boym, "From the Russian Soul to Post-Communist Nostalgia", *Representations* 49 (1995): 133–66, 133.
4 Boym, "From the Russian Soul", 133.
5 Fredrickson, "Vision and Material Practice", 49, 60.
6 Vladimir Tatlin, quoted by Kiaer, *Imagine no Possessions*, 44.
7 Fredrickson, "Vision and Material Practice", 52.
8 Kiaer, *Imagine no Possessions*, 70–71.
9 Kiaer, *Imagine no Possessions*, 46; Fredrickson, "Vision and Material Practice", 59.
10 Liubov Popova, "The Question of the New Methodology of Instruction (First Discipline of the Basic Department of the Vkhutemas Painting Faculty)", in *Liubov Popova*, eds. Dmitri V. Sarabianov and Natalia L. Adaskina (New York: Harry N. Abrams, 1990), 375–377, 375.
11 Liubov Popova, "The Essence of the Disciplines" in *Liubov Popova*, eds. Dmitri V. Sarabianov and Natalia L. Adaskina (New York: Harry N. Abrams, 1990), 369–371.
12 Maria Gough, "Faktura", 52.
13 Walter Benjamin, "The Work of Art in the Age of Mechanical Reproduction", in *Illuminations*, ed. Hannah Arendt, trans. Harry Zohn (New York: Schocken, 1969), 6.
14 Benjamin, "The Work of Art", 6.

15 Walter Benjamin, "The Work of Art in the Age of Its Technological Reproducibility: Second Version", in *The Work of Art in the Age of Its Technological Reproducibility and Other Writings on Media*, eds. Michael W. Jennings, Bridgid Doherty, and Thomas Y. Levin, trans. Edmund Jephcott, Rodney Livingstone, Howard Eiland, and others (Cambridge: Harvard University Press, 2008), 19–55, 26.

16 Daniel Mourenza, "Dreams of a Better Nature: Walter Benjamin on the Creation of a Collective Techno-Body", *Teknokultura: Revista de Cultura Digital y Movimientos Sociales* 10, no. 3 (2013): 693–718, quote on 701.

17 See also Mourenza, "Dreams of a Better Nature", 706.

18 Feminist theologian Mary Daly described God as a verb in *Beyond God the Father* (1973) to avoid gendered conceptualizations of the divine. In her later work she even replaced the word *God* with *Verb*. Laurel C. Schneider, "The Courage to See and to Sin: Mary Daly's Elemental Transformation of Paul Tillich's Ontology", in *Feminist Interpretations of Mary Daly*, eds. Sarah Lucia Hoagland and Marilyn Frye (University Park: Pennsylvania State University Press, 2000), 55–75, 61.

19 See also Catherine de Zegher, "A Century Under the Sign of Line: Drawing and Its Extensions (1910–2010)", in *On Line: Drawing Through the Twentieth Century*, eds. Cornelia H. Butler and Catherine de Zegher (New York: Museum of Modern Art, 2010), 47. Zegher underlines both the industrial and the laboratory connotations in Popova's use of lines, indicating a relationship between the artist and her work in which the artist discovers rather than designs, then constructs with the material at hand—not in order to express her own intention but in order to make the material functional.

20 Sarabianov, "Painting", 137. See also my comments on Spira in Chapter 1: "Backdrop".

21 Sarabianov, "Painting", 142.

22 Yablonskaya, *Women Artists of Russia's New Age*, 103, 109.

23 Popova, "On a Precise Criterion", 380.

24 Christine Blaettler, "Phantasmagoria: A Profane Phenomenon as a Critical Alternative to the Fetish", *Image and Narrative* 13, no. 1 (2012): 32–47, 38.

25 Blaettler, "Phantasmagoria", 44–45.

26 Fredrickson, "Vision and Material Practice", 56, 70.

27 See, for example, Fredrickson's discussion of Tatlin's flying machine *Letatlin*, in Fredrickson, "Vision and Material Practice", 67–71.

28 For image, see Fredrickson, "Vision and Material Practice", 62.

29 Fredrickson, "Vision and Material Practice", 63.

30 Kiaer, *Imagine no Possessions*, 125.

31 See image in Kiaer, *Imagine no Possessions*, 128–129.

32 Kiaer, *Imagine no Possessions*, 89.

33 Christina Lodder, "Liubov Popova: From Painting to Textile Design", *Tate Papers*, no. 14 (Autumn 2010); https://www.tate.org.uk/research/publications/tate-papers /14/liubov-popova-from-painting-to-textile-design, accessed 13 June 2019.

34 Benjamin, "The Work of Art", second version, 45.

35 Mourenza, "Dreams of a Better Nature", 706.

36 M. I. Franklin discusses the connections between Haraway's cyborg manifesto and Benjamin's work of art essay in "Reading Walter Benjamin and Donna Haraway in the Age of Digital Reproduction", *Information, Communication and Society* 5, no. 4 (2010): 591–624.

4   The Christ machine

At the close of the last chapter, we approached the idea of a second theology modelled on Benjamin's notion of second technology. A second theology, I suggested, would focus not on Christian truth as such but on the relationship between humanity and the ideas of Christian truth. A second theology would be more of a construction site than an archaeological site: a sort of workshop, perhaps. Shelves lined with boxes containing the elements of Christianity, tins holding theological tools; elements and tools often mixed up in the same container. As when processing a piece of wood or plastic, the constructor would need to know the characteristics of the material, its history, its possibilities and limitations, its way of functioning. But not with an aim to "restore" it, to turn it into what it was "meant" to be—that would be a task for first theology—nor to transform the elements beyond recognition to fulfil an already predetermined purpose. Rather, the aim is to be affected by them, to learn from their texture and also to assist them, make them functional wherever they are needed, to release them from their boxes, living and resilient, as resources for further reconstruction.

In this chapter, as part of our search for a constructive and relational approach to reality, in counterpoint to the well-known image of the face of Christ, I explore the image of Christ as machine. Thus, I attempt daringly to *do* second theology. Rather than ground my theological suggestions purely historically in the sources, in the origin as is theological custom, I endeavour to construct with three realities at hand—the Christ, the exclusive aspect of the Christ figure, and the machine—and in doing so I invite Gilles Deleuze and Felix Guattari into the workshop. Taking Haraway's critique of Deleuze and Guattari into regard, however, these two co-workers are not necessarily skilled for the task. Their notion of the machine is complemented by Popova's actual machinic construction for the production of *The Magnanimous Cuckold* (1922) by Vsvevolod Meyerhold (1874–1940). Finally, the bits and pieces brought together will manufacture a celestial machine complementing the beloved image of the face of Christ.

From face to machine

"Everyone knows Jesus: he is the most painted figure in all of world art, identifiable everywhere", states Joan Taylor in her introduction to the history of Jesus' imagery.[1] The image of Jesus's face, a basically similar prototype from the sixth century onwards, is known from innumerable portraits of an always recognisable face. The features are notably important and universally the same: the almond-shaped eyes, high cheekbones, slim face. Symbols and attributes are hardly needed to indicate his identity, even in early portraits from the sixth century one immediately recognises who it is. Deleuze and Guattari even draw on this historical fact when suggesting a philosophical consequence of the notion of the face. The face of Christ, they argue, is the face with which we compare all other faces. The Christ image—which has become the face of faces—embodies goodness, whiteness and maleness inseparably; it is the face of the White Man himself.[2] For Deleuze and Guattari, in other words, the face of Christ is the very basis for the universalization of white maleness; not only does it instigate this particular ideal, but it also serves as a ground for the notion of the human ideal as such. The face grounds the very idea of a correlate and its deviation. A face is limiting and excluding, they reason, by always instigating an either/or—either *this* or *that*—for example, either man or woman, either rich or poor, either black or white: "Aha, it's not a man and it's not a woman, so it must be a transvestite!"[3] The either/or easily falls into judgement; the face grounds identity and begets a *yes* or *no*, thus forming a ground on which to judge. The binary relation may just as easily mark a tolerance as indicate an enemy to be mowed down at all costs, they state.

In contrast to the notion of the face, Deleuze and Guattari introduce the notion of *the machine*. A machine, as opposed to a face, does not indicate a singular identity but points to a multiplicity of components. While the face indicates the *one*, the machine indicates the *many* pieces brought together in its construction. If the face indicates an origin, a birth, as well as an end, the machine indicates an ongoing process of creation. On the basis of this critique of the face of Christ by Deleuze and Guattari, this chapter elaborates the symbol of the cross—the crucifixion event—as machine. I explore the multiplicity rather than the singular identity of the Christ notion; the ongoing construction and relational aspect rather than the origin-telos spectrum. My intention is, in other words, to do second theology by way of the Christ figure and the machine. After staying with Deleuze and Guattari a little longer, we turn to the critique put forward by Haraway.

In *Anti-Oedipus*, when introducing one of their notions of the machine— *the desiring machines*—Deleuze and Guattari write:

We live today in the age of partial objects, bricks that have been shattered to bits, and leftovers. We no longer believe in the myth of the existence of fragments that, like pieces of an antique statue, are merely waiting for the last one to be turned up, so that they may all be glued back together to create a unity that is precisely the same as the original unity.[4]

The notion of the one origin is lost, they argued in 1972. The very idea that the past can be recovered, or that identity is singular, is lost for their historical era. "We no longer believe in a primordial totality that once existed, or in a final totality that awaits us at some future day", they continue. Neither the past or the future will provide us with a unity that explains it all, no point where it all comes together: "We no longer believe in the dull grey outlines of a dreary, colourless dialectic of evolution, aimed at forming a harmonious whole out of heterogeneous bits by rounding off their rough edges. We believe only in totalities that are peripheral".

This is to say, there may be totalities, systems, theories or organisations that form a whole, a unity, but their organisation is contingent, changeable and consisting of separate pieces:

And if we discover such a totality alongside various separate parts, it is a whole of these particular parts but does not unify them; rather, it is added to them as a new part fabricated separately.[5]

Machines, in Deleuze and Guattari's account, are constructions of separate parts. The construction does not unite the parts, but organises them. The construction as such finally indicates nothing but construction itself, the possibility to construct and construction as immanent action. A machine is not a given, it is a construction: an organisation of separate elements. A machine is made up of partial objects, forming a whole out of heterogeneous bits—not because they belong together inherently, not because they were "meant" for each other, but because creation is possible, construction is possible.

If the image of Jesus' face has remained largely the same from the sixth century to the present day, it follows according to Deleuze and Guattari's analysis of the face that representational identity has been used to denote the kernel of Christian faith during that same period. Throughout the history of art, artists have endeavoured to break with the logic of depiction and representation: to question in different ways the very idea that there is a "true" reality that may be depicted, or that the reality depicted is "more real" than the reality created on the canvas. But the constructivists went further than most in this regard. In Popova's artistic vision, construction was taken up to replace representation in art; the notion of depiction should give way, in her regard, to a notion of ongoing construction. The infinite potentialities to construct anew out of the very elements of life was at the heart of her artistic endeavour.

Deleuze and Guattari's critique of representation, sketched above, turns into a concrete artistic practice with Popova. In the history of art, Popova observes, there has been a gradual development away from representation and depiction, which at one stage led to what she describes as the distortion of elements (she exemplifies this stage with Picasso's works), but distortion was just a stage. This distortion of elements led to a *transformation* of the very understanding of elements, or of that which makes up the object as object.[6] As director of the Inkhuk in Moscow, Popova repeatedly argues that elements should no longer be regarded as pieces of an object—pieces that one can take apart and put together slightly differently, thus still relating them to the original object—but as coincidental parts. In Popova's words:

> The object as such is no longer studied and depicted, only the separate formal elements on which it can be laid out and from which it is composed; only that which defines the concept of the object and not all the elements in order of their existence in the object. The artist has gone from an imagination-depiction of the object to an analysis of the concepts comprising the object's essence.[7]

To acknowledge the potentialities of objects, we must study them closely, bit by bit, until they reappear beyond our expectations.

Applying Popova's account of representation to the depiction of Jesus accordingly, to re-interpret the face of Christ—to "rearrange" it in the sense of depicting it outside the common norms and expectations—is important and parallels the cubist distortion of perspectives. Yet for Popova distortion was just a stage on the way to transformation, since distortion still related to the object rather than to its separable components. Subsequently, interpretational twists in relation to the face of Jesus might momentarily open up new images of *the face of faces*, yet they inevitably evoke the original from which they deviate. Distortions of the face risk letting the original face, which we know so well, stand forth as precisely that: as the original norm in relation to which the variation is an exception. In line with Popova's constructivist thinking, however, the face of faces should not only be distorted but completely transformed by attention paid to the parts of its construction—and to the possibility of construction as such. What does that mean in practice, though? And is a machine necessarily more liberating than a face? Do we not need faces, do we not need face-to-face and nose-to-nose encounters?

Haraway, Deleuze and dogs

In *A Thousand Plateaus*, Deleuze and Guattari introduce the notion of becoming-animal.[8] It is a notion arising from the insight that the Kantian autonomous subject in fact involves a crack—the subject is split at its very centre by its interior hearing of the voice of the self, and of others, commanding the law. The human subject is not singular, not universal, because it consists of the many voices and memories that speak in it: my past self is constantly produced through the simple fact of time passing, my ageing; my past self is also constantly produced by the others and the memories that inhabit me. Becoming is a never-ending production of the self as multiplicity, hence becoming is never about becoming Man, becoming Subject, but always about becoming minor—about passing over into others, into differences. As I age, I do not become more myself in the sense of a more and more intact subject, but quite the opposite. I multiply with every experience. Becoming is thus also about *becoming-animal*, about noting the animals in me, not becoming like them, not them becoming like me, but letting their voices in me tell a tale that makes me think otherwise. If I let them, that is. If I recognise the becoming in me, if I recognise the other voices, then the animal voices can help me think differently. To do so, to recognise the becoming in me, to write and think becoming, *to write like a rat*, changes the world. Becoming-animal is a passing over into difference, not an arrival or an imitation. It is not, therefore, the establishment of a relationship between a human and an animal—because such an account would presuppose an intact subject, a subject without a crack.

Donna Haraway's notion of *becoming-with* as the way of being among *critters* in the *Chthulucene* vaguely resembles Deleuze and Guattari's notion of *becoming-animal*—but for Haraway a mere resemblance is all there is.[9] Even if she explicitly acknowledges the inspiration of Deleuze, she would not trust him or Guattari to help us construct a proper material theology—if by that we mean a theology that truly engages with species and matter, or at least opens us up to such engagement. Haraway had hoped to find an ally in Deleuze and Guattari's becoming-animal for the task of companion species, she writes, but found herself wanting to announce: "Ladies and Gentlemen, behold, the enemy!"[10] She explicates her sympathy towards their endeavour at large, their critique of the individuated Oedipal subject and the way it affects culture, politics and philosophy—and the later Haraway does "write like a rat" in the sense of letting the rat-voices in her tell the tales that change the world, I find, just as Deleuze and Guattari envision.[11] Notwithstanding this sympathy, her problem with them begins with the elevation of anomaly as that which escapes the norm-contra-abnorm dualism, the molar unities having to give way to molecular multiplicities, the opposition they posit between becoming and filiation. The anomalous is for them "neither an individual nor a species", it is a multiplicity and as such is defined not by extension or by the elements that compose it but by its "intension", its intensities, its affects.[12]

The alliance between Captain Ahab and the white whale Moby Dick, which Deleuze and Guattari use to exemplify a becoming-animal, is a good example in their eyes precisely because it is an alliance with anomaly as intension. It is a bordering that loosens the subject/object distinction, but does so not through an *actual* encounter between a human and another organism but through an indulgence in the hunt for that which is not categorised: the anomalous, or *becoming* as such. Haraway finds such a description of becoming to be the opposite of her becoming-with, simply because it finally disregards the actual entanglement with the mundane, the ordinary and with actual animals. "This is a philosophy of the sublime", she writes, "not the earthly, not the mud; becoming-animal is not an autre-mondialisation".[13] Anyone who has read Haraway on her canine friend Cayenne would know that Deleuze and Guattari lost her in writing "Ahab's Moby-Dick is not like the little cat or dog owned by an elderly woman who honors and cherishes it"—which Haraway admits is what she experienced[14]—not only due to personal insult, however, but because of the disengagement with actual living individuals that it implies.

In my view, Deleuze and Guattari's becoming-animal presents a way of thinking and writing that I believe could change the world. Leonard Lawlor tells it beautifully in his essay "Following the Rats", suggesting that writing like a rat—acknowledging the animals/voices/differences close to me, in me, among whom I am constantly becoming—would call forth a new kind of collectivity.[15] It would be a writing struggling to escape the dominant forms of expression, thus a writing that could produce a people, a democracy, with a very different relation to other species and organisms than we have.

The aged Lord Chandos, writing a letter to Francis Bacon whom he has not met for twenty-six years, wonders: Am I still the same person your letter addresses? He does not think so because ageing does things, changes things, living and encountering changes things. Chandos had distributed rat poison in the cellar of one of his dairy farms (not for the first time, one must assume): "Towards evening I had gone off for a ride and, as you can imagine, thought no more about it". But then it struck him:

> There suddenly loomed up before me the vision of that cellar, resounding with the death-struggle of a mob of rats. I felt everything within me: the cool, musty air of the cellar filled with the sweet and pungent reek

of poison, and the yelling of the death cries breaking against the mold-
ering walls; the vain convulsions of those convoluted bodies as they
tear about in confusion and despair; their frenzied search for escape,
and the grimace of icy rage when a couple collide with one another at
a blocked-up crevice.

The rat agony was suddenly real in him—"within me, the soul of this animal
bared its teeth to its monstrous fate"[16]—not as a pity, but as an inescapable,
immense sympathy. Deleuze and Guattari describe it as a decisive experience: after it you either attempt to write like a rat, simply to be able to share
your experience, or you stop writing. Either you allow the thought that is in
you but not you—not who you thought you were, yet nonetheless there—to
be expressed or you turn silent. Not because you have understood the rat
experience in the cellar, of course you haven't; not because you assume the
rats experienced what you experienced; but because of the undeniable presence in your body of that which you formerly regarded as not-you, not-man,
not-human. Either you stop writing, stop thinking, or you write like the rat
in you, think like the rat in you. And if you do, it will change your thinking
and writing, and others' as well.

Still, Haraway does have a point. Lord Chandos' letter is fictive, written
by Hugo von Hofmannsthal, and Ahab and Moby Dick are fictive. Deleuze
and Guattari write about them in their ninety-seven-page chapter in which
there are in fact no *actual* animals, humans, relations or faces—other than
the idealised face of Jesus. The chapter is finally about writing and thinking, about fiction, about tales that could change the world, and not about
the actual messiness of relationships. Not even about the messiness of trying to realise one's ideas. Not about what happens when my thoughts turn
into actual constructions that people interact with. Not what happens in the
becoming-with over which I have finally only very little control—a reality
that might lead me as far away from the repressive conformity as I wanted
or might lead me right back to where I was. And if the writing and thinking relates only indirectly to the actual world, then it most likely will not
change it.

Still, change is a messy and difficult task. When art becomes political in
Benjamin's sense—meaning active, productive, more verb than noun, producing rather than reproducing—what can happen? Adhering to Haraway's
critique, let us take a look into the dirty business of realising one's ideas.
Before returning to the Christ figure, we shall consider an immensely suc-
cessful yet disturbing theatre production revolving around a machine, and
around letting go of representation in order to open up to construction and
to the realities of becoming.

The stage machine

In 1921, the Russian theatre director, actor and producer Vsevolod Meyerhold was to put up a large, innovative, even groundbreaking theatre production at a mass festival on Khodinskoe Field. Moscow was organising the Third Congress of the Communist International and the experimental, inventive producer planned a large-scale theatrical festival to go with it. At the end of the festivities an interactive play entitled *The Struggle and Victory of the Soviets* was to be performed on the field—not held inside a golden decorated bourgeoise theatre, but brought out to the people. Symbolism was important, as was military action and machine constructions. Two large monumental structures were to be built, one representing "The Fortress of Capital", the other representing "The City of the Future". There was to be an actual battle, an attack on the fortress of capital, a struggle in fire and light, and finally victory, slogans written on the factory wall such as: "Put what workers' hands make into workers hands!" The actors dressed as workers, peasants and soldiers, tanks, cars, motorcycles would finally conquer and, together with the audience, approach the other construction: the city of the future. Spotlights would create a light curtain, an orchestra would play, aeroplanes would fly over the scene and light it up with searchlights beaming slogans against the forest and the future city construction before the grand finale: Fireworks, of course, and the orchestra now playing "The Internationale"! End of festival.[17]

It never took place, though. In the year 1921, famine struck Russia and the government prohibited expensive festivals and celebrations. But the never-actualised production somehow lived on. The idea kept on inspiring creative notions that theatre could be different—performed outdoors on an open field, including slogans and large symbolic constructions—that theatre could leave the purely relational and psychological, that it could be political and productive. In Meyerhold's vision, the light beaming from spotlights and projectors played a crucial part in the political theatre production, and so did the machine-like structures symbolising the two cities. Trying to imagine a time when this theatrical vision of Meyerhold was fresh, when all the ideas were new, including the vision of a victorious working class—I try to imagine a situation in which his production actually seemed like a good and groundbreaking idea. It is almost impossible. Yet we know that Meyerhold was finally too innovative, too artistically and theoretically bold for the dreadful regime that was to get an increasingly harsh grip over Russia in the years to come. Meyerhold was killed in 1938.[18]

From Popova's point of view, Meyerhold's later offer to collaborate in the production of Belgian playwright Fernand Crommelynck's *The*

Magnanimous Cuckold did not seem uninviting. She was asked to design the costumes and build the scenic construction for the production. Popova shared certain ideas in common with Meyerhold's theatrical vision such as the merging of old and new, and especially the idea that the artistic task was more about production, construction and expediency than about aesthetics, stylistic ideals and theories. Meyerhold thought the artist should move from depicting the object to real, hands-on construction in space.[19] Popova's canvases that same year were filled with constructions, what she called her spatial force constructions. They were two-dimensional architectonic constructions made up of what resembled rays, beams and circling passer-whirlwinds. Hence, the idea of creating a three-dimensional version of what she was already pursuing in her paintings may have been tempting. As we have seen, Meyerhold had planned to use rays, spotlight beams, in his grand open-field production and Popova used rays in her later architectonic paintings, as an incorporeal and even spiritual building material.

There were many points of connection, yet she was reluctant. Though I would like to think her hesitation related in part to the tackiness of Meyerhold's never-actualised production described above and to the despicable story told in Crommelynck's play, that is probably not true. More likely, she was reluctant because she was surrounded by her fellow constructivists, who were forming their ideas and identity as a group, and what they did—what any one of them did—was important to all of them. She had already been mocked for being too *bourgeoise*, having been brought up in a wealthy family.[20] Art historians Natalia Adaskina and Elena Rakitin both convincingly argue that she hesitated because of where she was artistically and intellectually at the time.[21] She had decided to leave easel painting behind in the spring of 1921; she was dissatisfied with creating purely artistic objects and wanted instead to create for life, for concrete production. The theatre construction she was asked to create was three-dimensional, a large-scale machine-like construction and as such part of a project in which theatre was seen as productive rather than merely aesthetic or simply amusing. It was concrete, but nonetheless it was theatre—an artistic laboratory, not real life—which is why she hesitated before taking the offer.

Christopher Baugh contextualises *The Magnanimous Cuckold* of 1922 as part of the development of theatre at the time through the notion of the theatre as machine: the stage machine. Through Meyerhold's theatrical vision the stage was stripped, liberated from everything pertaining to a naturalistic theatre, with its aim to mimic and aestheticise. At the Moscow Art Theatre, Meyerhold had gotten rid of the painted cardboard models that would turn the stage into an aesthetic vision of what the performance depicted, and instead laid the stage bare.[22] "As we turned those models over", Meyerhold explained,

> we seemed to be holding the entire contemporary theatre in our hands. In our desire to burn and destroy them we were already close to the desire to destroy the obsolete methods of the naturalistic theatre.[23]

Popova's assignment was to make a construction for Meyerhold's naked stage—a stage which was equally transparent as regards the mechanics of the theatre: the innovation was not about hiding the production process but laying it bare. It was not about mimicking, representing, depicting, but about producing and constructing, so she decided to do it.

Popova's machine was made of timber, metal components, minimal paint, a schematic windmill, ladders, wheels, ramps, delivery chutes, a large black wheel with the letters CR-ML-NCK (indicating the playwright's name) turning in the back, rhythmically moving with the actors. At least in theory. Rather than being inactive, a merely aesthetical or illustrative backdrop, actors interacted with the machine—walked, ran and slid on it, manipulated it in their performance—and yet the machine assisted rather than dominated

Figure 4.1 Stage design for the theatre play the Magnanimous Cuckold (1922)

Figure 4.2 Production clothing for actor no. 5 (1921)

the performance. The actors were having fun with it. Indeed, the entire performance indicated that productive, hyperefficient work in a transparent
production process was fun. Being a machine together with the machine,
interacting, letting matter be as active as oneself, was fun. And the horrific

black-humoured story underscored the socialist vision of a society with no possessions. *The Magnanimous Cuckold* is the story of a jealous husband who shares his wife, eventually, with every man in the village to test her fidelity. In a sense, it is about desire as transparent machinery, collectivity as commonality. The husband's riotous possessiveness finally upsets and disrupts the entire village, to the point that the village women turn against the wife, and the men turn against Bruno, the cuckold himself. Jealousy destroys the man and drives the wife away. It is, in short, a story about yet another dreadful fate for women, yet another man and his deviant—to speak with Deleuze and Guattari in terms of correlate and its deviation—and even, as well, a story about man and his possessiveness. And it is supposed to be fun. Though I would like to think that the well-known egalitarian companionship among the men and women of Russian constructivism during these years opened positions from which it would be natural to react against such symbolic use of women in a play, I have found no such evidence.[24]

However, paradoxically, the production of *The Magnanimous Cuckold* proved a success, played for a long time, and did nothing less than secure Popova's name in the history of art and create what Rakitin calls the "Popova canon". The influence of Popova's stage machine was later directly noticeable in Aleksandr Vesnin's maquette for a G. K. Chesterton play, in Gustav Klutsis' street construction projects and in the way students in Rodchenko's workshop exhibited their work.[25] Her costume designs, as already mentioned, were pioneering. Popova consciously strove for androgyny, saying she had "a fundamental disinclination to making any distinction between the men's and women's costumes". *Production Clothing for Actor no. 5* (1921) shows one of the female actors' costumes: a plain blue workers overalls-style dress with a big black apron shaped like a black rectangle recalling Malevich's black square.

The costumes for female actors barely differed from those of the male actors. Kiaer describes this bold, androgynous design: "As good an icon as any for the new Soviet woman emancipated by Bolshevism, shedding the trappings of bourgeois femininity and becoming a productive worker equal to men". Kiaer notes that the life of the equal Russian woman was short (and illustrates this by comparing a poster by Stepanova to a later poster by Maria Bri-Bein). In the mid 1930s, the state ideology reverted to a more "traditional, feminine and motherly" ideal of "limited equality".[26]

Yet the immediate reaction to Popova's contribution was an accusation of artistic plagiarism. Painter Georgii Yakulov was doggedly convinced that the bold scenographical ideas in her scene constructions "would never have occurred to a Soviet mademoiselle like Popova", and he suggested that she had stolen ideas from two younger artists: the brothers Vladimir and Georgii Stenberg.[27] Since Popova had to respond, a meeting was held to dispute the matter; the discussion concluded against Yakulov's assertions and Popova was acquitted of his charges and the originality of her work was confirmed.[28] What is more interesting for our purposes is the debate that arose in the aftermath of her contribution in the circles at the Inkhuk. This discussion took up the array of issues that many argue spurred her own initial doubts: What would a theatrical constructivism be? Could the constructivism that only a year earlier had rejected easel-painting for the purpose of real-life objects be expressed in a theatrical design, and still remain true to its mission? Another gathering was organised in April 1922 to discuss the matter. Popova's way of handling the situation, illustrating what can happen when ideas meet reality, are interesting for our purposes.

Popova first emphasises that she does not "pretend to any final or even generally positive resolution of the problems posed".[29] She affirms her intent to remain within the theoretical framework that the constructivists have agreed on, suggesting the problems discussed should be dealt with not on an aesthetic level but on the level of the actual production process: "to deal with the question differently from its usual aesthetic resolution, completely on another plane, with the goal of resolving the tasks exclusively with respect to the given production and its means and aims".[30] Her theoretical conviction is advanced as a practical act. She sums up what she aimed to do personally and professionally: "to equip the theatrical action with its material elements".[31] In the actual context of her practical action, however, her idea of treating theory as practice was being obstructed. Things simply did not work out the way she wanted because at times, for instance, the wheels of her construction would not turn. She describes how she had to fight "outmoded aesthetic customs and criteria"; how the "farcical character" of the action, which lent everything an aesthetic character, made it hard to view it as a strict work process; how the work uniform was difficult to design because it had to be able to do so much; there were problems with the painting and with the equipment at large; and the actors did not have time to rehearse sufficiently with the scenography. In short, the inexpedient *realities* of machinic theatre production displaced her expedient *theory* of it—and the notion of a machine co-working with the actor-workers was abandoned. She could not do what she wanted even when all she wanted was *doing*. The idea of an art that *does*—art that has gone from depicting to composing to constructing—was not all that easy to realise. The *idea* of action is not action itself—just as the *idea* of the dog-human relationship is not the same as a dog-human relationship, which is why Deleuze and Guattari do have a point when they suggest their becoming-animal finally has to be about writing and thinking, not about actual encounters.

Adaskina stresses that what makes Popova's contribution to *The Magnanimous Cuckold* outstanding is precisely the energy that emerged from the many compromises, the manner in which it challenged the neatness of the creative ideas behind it. Its import lay in "the destruction of unified theoretical postulates, in the vital pulsing of creative energy destroying and facilitating the schematism of the original goals".[32] The fact that reality challenged Popova's notion of reality secured the greatness of the production as a whole. We have a production about production that, in sum, shows us that production is not merely that; there are intertwined levels of ideas, customs and practical circumstances that render theatre production more complex and fraught than it would seem *prima facie*. The theatre machine, in other words, is more entangled and complex than the stage machine. This was also a production about abuse of women that, paradoxically, placed a woman in the history books. In this creative attempt to get rid of theory as a heavenly superstructure, letting theory be displaced with action, action escaped the notion of action itself. It revealed the messiness of construction as a complex mishmash of ideas, practicalities, desire and other thingies—including utopias. Even if Popova herself does not seem to come to this conclusion, her opening of the discussion indicates that the problems that arise when theory meets practice cannot simply be resolved. Though it is in perfect congruence with her thinking at large, she is too caught up in the orthodoxy of constructivism to see it. She is not able to realise that the machine that she, the actors, Meyerhold, the room, the paint, the technical devices and the play create is greater than them, partly beyond their control—and as such is precisely a machine in Deleuze and Guattari's sense. Her constructivist ideas and her attempt at materialising them render her more mature as a constructor than she is as a thinker.

To invoke Popova as a source of inspiration for political theology is thus at once questionable and important for several reasons, but for one reason in particular: as a key voice in the Russian avantgarde she supported the Russian revolution; she was happy about it, believed in it. She did not live to see the terrible consequences, as she died of scarlet fever in 1924. Artists like her later had to flee from Russia, as nonobjective art was banned in 1932, yet we do not know if her ideas would have made a difference—there is no vaccine against totalitarianism. Despite her conviction concerning construction as an ongoing action in the elements of the world itself, she was unable to recognise that this conviction was in fact confirmed by the happenings around *The Magnanimous Cuckold*. This is to say, she was too caught up in the theoretical assumptions of construction to note the confirmation of her conviction happening around her, in part happening beyond her control. She supported the people's revolt against the tsarist establishment, but the people eventually ended up with a more totalitarian regime than the one they had overthrown and left behind. It is vital to keep the result in mind, and to digest the ideas that enabled it, because Popova's time resembles ours in the sense that it is a time of in-between in which old authorities are weakened, questioned, and the political scene is changing and open to change. Popova was desperate for new political solutions, for a vision of the future, and she proposed a way forward from her artistic perspective: a humble approach to the elements of reality in order to take part in the ongoing construction of the world, and to explore yet unseen possibilities and potentialities of the materials. Still, the humble conviction of playing the role of matter's assistant was humbler in theory than in practice.

The celestial machine

Let us now take up and apply these insights with respect to imagery of the Christian theological tradition which, complementing the image of Jesus' face, could open up theology to the notion of an ongoing construction—a notion that, in turn, may open theology towards theopolitical activism. According to Giorgio Agamben, the notion of the machine is not new to Christian theology; it was used in early Christianity to designate the cross event. Pseudo-Athanasius and Ignazio of Antioch, he argues, used the notion of the *celestial machine* to describe the cross, the cross as machine.[33] The expression *celestial machine* derives from the ancient *mechane* (source of the English word *machine*), which was a construction at the ancient Greek theatre: a wooden arm that lifted a god onto the stage. The *mechane* lifted the god or god-actor up from behind the scene, lowered him or her into the actors' midst and then—once the plot was reconfigured by the divine presence—the *mechane* lifted the god back up off the stage until the next dramatic visitation. The expression *deus ex machina*, or "god from the machine"—an expression used in literature and filmmaking to designate the unexpected rescuer, the saviour suddenly placed in the hopeless reality of the main characters—invokes this stage machine, also referred to as the *celestial machine*. According to Agamben, the *celestial machine*, with connotations of this Greek theatre construction, was brought into early Christian theology as a reference to 1 Cor 4:9: "We have become a theatre for the world, of angels and human beings".[34]

Would it make a difference if we were to think of Christ as machine rather than face? If the kernel of Christianity were described through mechanical imagery rather than figurative depiction? Is not a face also a machine in the sense that it is made up of heterogeneous bits, of fragments, experience, memories, hopes, genes and scars? Well yes—and again, theological construction is not about replacing but adding, not about deleting the face but rather complementing it with the machine. It is an addition that could activate currently less active Christian functions; it is an addition that may help us see the entire wood, not just the trees singled out by Christian orthodoxy. Thus, it could help us see the plurality, feel the multiplicity, hear the noisiness of Christianity that opens to a more plural Christian thinking and acting that may change the world.

First, if Christ is a machine—a celestial machine—rather than a face, then Christ, conceived as event, becomes action and verb rather than identity. The cross event of Christ as celestial machine *is* what it *does*—constantly moving, stuck in its repetitious motion, persistently repeating its motion of sinking/rising, dying/resurrecting through history, through liturgy, through theological analysis, in art as well as in collective and individual experiences of faith. It is even effective way beyond what we think it does—or want it to do.

Second, the repetition of the cross event is a repetition of *difference*, an assemblage of Christian expressions. Not a repetition of the original event connected to the one recognisable identity, but a perpetual event recognisable through its action, its motion and transformation.

Third, following Popova, we as second-theology mechanics or second-theology constructors may take part in the constructing. We may take part and take apart, deconstruct theological constructions, piece by piece; analyse them in the laboratories: what is it *to die, to sink, to rise, to live*, if we take one gear, one plank at a time? What is it to sink if detached from the possibility of rising, what is it to rise detached from the possibility of sinking? What is it *to live* without *to die*? What is it to repeat without death, without the end of repetition? What is movement? What is movement without height and depth? And what are the bits and pieces of the cross event in the Christian narratives, in the liturgies, the histories of theology, in the stories we tell, in the artefacts, the prayers, what are they in the multiplicity of Christian traditions? Then, to reconstruct, to nail movement onto dying, to hammer rising onto repeating, to glue living onto sinking, knowing that in the end, we do not know what our doing does. Perhaps also to dig deep in the old elements, unveil fragments of constructivism in the Christian past, as with the symbol of the *Ichthys* wheel, earlier than the face, from a time when depiction of a face was not only limiting but possibly even blasphemous. In this symbol, the Greek letters of *Ichthys* are brought together constructing a wheel of the separate parts, with the cross at its centre as one element among several.

Inspired by the critique of representation developed outside the theological sphere in the twentieth century, we may unearth analogous notions in the history of theology, where the discussion of the possibility to depict the divine has been an ongoing debate. Here I have suggested only two such notions as examples—the celestial machine and the *Ichthys* wheel—but there are many more to be uncovered or constructed. Whether it begets a transformation or merely a distortion, experimenting with theological notions as a constructivist practice, with the cross as a *celestial machine*, does open new spaces for theological thought. Through the notion of the cross as a die-and-live-again-machine, forever repeating death-and-life, forever killing God, forever reviving God in this world—a repetitious death and resurrection repeated in infinite varieties in theology, art, music, film and church life—Christ stands forth as an immanent and concrete movement with incalculable, infinite implications.

If there is no origin, no original identity in the sense of a norm in relation to which new expressions multiply variations, are there no limits? Is not reality as machine, Christianity as machine, open to anything? Well, possibly. A quick look around at the contemporary political reality, with its many different Christian alliances within the political right as well as the left, suggests that might be so. *The Magnanimous Cuckold* of 1922 suggests the same. There is, as above, no vaccine against totalitarianism; it may grow in Christian theology, in communism, constructivism, Trumpism, Deleuzianism and so on. But *if* that is where a second theology were to end up, it would be because it had forgotten the core principle we have suggested thus far: the one principle shared by Popova, Haraway, and Deleuze and Guattari, which is simply that construction is the only given. If we are to take part in such theological construction, we must acquire a deep humility in relation to construction as such, its endless possibilities and also, Popova would add, in relation to the elements. A deep acquaintance with what constitutes us, our space, volume, colour, weight as well as the fragments of knowledge, the bits of world, historical, political and theological leftovers that make up our thinking. A deep humility in the relation to the other organisms, the actual faces, bodies, the matter that constitutes our shared lifeworld, beginning with the matter at hand. Writing and thinking like a rat.

For us as theological constructors, the material with which we work are the texts, the liturgy, the dogma, the history, the experiences, the personal and collective narratives, voices and the elements they comprise. Only with a deep acquaintance with the expressions of Christianity can we truly begin to reorganise the fragments, while they of course reorganise us, whatever we were, reorganise our mechanic appearances and performances.

Notes

1　Joan E. Taylor, *What Did Jesus Look Like?* (London: Bloomsbury T & T Clark, 2018), 1.
2　Gilles Deleuze and Felix Guattari, *A Thousand Plateaus: Capitalism and Schizophrenia*, trans. Brian Massumi (London: Athlone, 1999), 177.
3　Deleuze and Guattari, *A Thousand Plateaus*, 177.
4　Gilles Deleuze and Felix Guattari, *Anti-Oedipus: Capitalism and Schizophrenia*, trans. Robert Hurley (London: Continuum, 2004), 45.

5 Deleuze and Guattari, *Anti-Oedipus*, 45–46.
6 Liubov Popova, "The Question of the New Methodology of Instruction", in *Liubov Popova*, eds. Dmitri V. Sarabianov and Natalia L. Adaskina (New York: Harry N. Abrams, 1990), 375–377, 376.
7 Popova, "The Question of the New Methodology", 375.
8 Deleuze and Guattari, *A Thousand Plateaus*, 232–309.
9 Haraway, *When Species Meet*, 27.
10 Haraway, *When Species Meet*, 27.
11 Haraway, *When Species Meet*, 27.
12 Deleuze and Guattari, *A Thousand Plateaus*, 245.
13 Haraway, *When Species Meet*, 28.
14 Haraway, *When Species Meet*, 30; Deleuze and Guattari, *A Thousand Plateaus*, 244. To Deleuze and Guattari, the relationship between Donna and Cayenne would most likely fall into the category of "playing Oedipus", playing family, "my little dog". Deleuze and Guattari, *A Thousand Plateaus*, 233.
15 Leonard Lawlor, "Following the Rats: An Essay on the Concept of Becoming-Animal in Deleuze and Guattari", *Sub-Stance* 37, no. 3(117) on "The Political Animal" (2008): 169–187.
16 Hugo von Hofmannsthal, "The Letter of Lord Chandos", trans. Tania Stern and James Stern, *Jubilat*, no. 11; http://www.jubilat.org/jubilat/archive/vol11/poem_10/.
17 Natalia Adaskina, "Part Two: Theory, Teaching, and Design", in *Liubov Popova*, eds. Dmitri V. Sarabianov and Natalia L. Adaskina, trans. Marian Schwartz (New York: Harry N. Abrams, 1990), 190–307, 249.
18 Edward Braun, *Meyerhold: A Revolution in Theatre* (Wallington: Methuen Drama, 1998), 306.
19 Adaskina, "Part Two", 251.
20 Sandqvist, *Det andra könet i öst*, 115.
21 Elena Rakitin, "How Meierkhol'd Never Worked with Tatlin, and What Happened as a Result", in *The Great Utopia: The Russian and Soviet Avantgarde 1915–1932*, ed. Catherine Cooke (New York: Guggenheim Museum, 1992), 650; Adaskina, "Part Two", 251.
22 Christopher Baugh, *Theatre, Performance and Technology: The Development and Transformation of Scenography* (Basingstoke: Palgrave Macmillan, 2013), 62.
23 Meyerhold, in Baugh, *Theatre, Performance and Technology*, 62.
24 See, for example, Christina Kiaer, "The Short Life of the Equal Woman: Remembering the Work of Russian Female Artists Under Stalin in the 1930s", in *TATE ETC.* (20 October 2017), https://www.tate.org.uk/tate-etc/issue-15-spring-2009/short-life-equal-women.
25 Rakitin, "How Meierkhol'd Never Worked with Tatlin", 650.
26 Kiaer, "The Short Life of the Equal Woman", n.p.
27 Adaskina, "Part Two: Theory, Teaching, and Design", 251.
28 Adaskina, "Part Two: Theory, Teaching, and Design", 251.
29 Popova, "Introduction to the Inkhuk Discussion", 378.
30 Popova, "Introduction to the Inkhuk Discussion", 378.
31 Popova, "Introduction to the Inkhuk Discussion", 378.
32 Adaskina, "Part Two", 253.
33 Giorgio Agamben, *The Mystery of Evil: Benedict and the End of Days*, trans. Adam Kotsko (Stanford: Stanford University Press, 2017), 32.
34 Agamben, *The Mystery of Evil*, 32.

5 Last thing(ie)s

Eschatology out of joint

The future is not what it used to be—space-age food pills and flying cars as one stage in the never-ending advancement of human progress. It is near and scary. The world expands for many of us, as we cease imagining that we could fly anywhere, while time shrinks. Space expands, time shrinks, yet our awareness of life in far-flung places is greater than ever. The climate crisis inevitably challenges habitual Christian ideas of time and space; or, as Catherine Keller succinctly puts it: "We had time".[1] Awareness of the condition of planet Earth inexorably calls for a focus on the current, on the next few years, on our actual material reality and its limits in time, while also opening our eyes to the disastrous worldwide effects of climate change.

This last chapter before our concluding manifesto explores eschatology through the notions of time and space in relation to the current situation. With an odd congregation of theology-mechanics we discuss the temporality of eschatology to finally suggest a radical material eschatology for second-theology constructors. The assembly is odd in the sense that it is hard to imagine the room in which these thinkers would ever meet—had they happened to be alive at the same time. Yet these are odd times, so we engage with (among others) Danish theologian Vitor Westhelle, Finish theologian Veli-Matti Kärkkäinen, Michel Foucault, Gilles Deleuze, Swedish theologian Sigurd Bergmann, Antonova, Benjamin Keller, and of course Popova.

The near and far

For a few years now, I have been teaching a course on the holy spirit. I did not create the course and was not thrilled when first asked to teach it. No continental philosophy in sight, just a straightforward Systematic Theology course on the third person of the trinity. Against all odds, however, the course itself and one of the course books, Veli-Matti Kärkkäinen's *The Holy Spirit and Salvation*, have become personal favourites. I will come back to why, but let me first discuss a disturbing aspect of the book. Structured like many theology overviews, the book begins with the history of Western and Eastern churches, then passes through the scholastics, the Renaissance, reformation movements ranging from moderate to radical, moves on to theological responses to modern thought, North American charismatic and evangelical movements, then critical theology including feminist theology and ecotheology, and finally, brought together in the last chapters is the rest of the world: African, Asian and South American theology. The rest of the world, it seems, did not really fit anywhere, so it was put last.

Danish theologian Vitor Westhelle suggests an explanation to why the South and the far East often stand forth as incompatible with Christian theology at large: it is a consequence of Christianity's fixation with temporality, he argues. The Western Christian preoccupation with time has made Western Christianity lose dimension, lose its sense of space. He quotes Native American theologian George E. Tinker, stating that "the western cultures in which the gospel has traditionally come to find its home are so fundamentally oriented toward temporality and disoriented from any foundational sense of spatiality".[2] The gospel is set in history, a story with a beginning, a middle and an end; thus a history from elsewhere, a story with a different beginning, middle and end necessarily challenges the gospel as traditionally conceived. The other story, the different story, needs to be placed within the history of Christianity—that is, the universal history of Christ eventuating in a universal history of humanity—or else it is simply not the gospel, not the history of salvation or the spirit's workings in the world as we know them. Christian thinkers—we systematic theologians in particular—look behind and look ahead, but to look sideways, well, such work tends to be labelled postcolonial. "The very idea of a universal history", Westhelle comments, "emerges as a Western idea and is not a universal one".[3]

We have heard that before, but what is new in Westhelle's reasoning is his pinpointing of the consequences of temporality finally outdoing spatiality in Christian thought. Westhelle could have started with the philosophy of history discussions after Karl Löwith's *Meaning in History* (1949) in which Löwith traced what he regarded as a destructive utopianism in the very notion of history from Jacob Burckhardt to the Bible. In fact, Westhelle could have written his entire study on the aftermath of that discussion on Christian temporality, yet he chooses to address it only indirectly. He touches on alternatives to Löwith's view as presented by thinkers like Jacob Taubes and Walter Benjamin (in whose *arcade* he ends up asking a beggar for the exit). These debates on the notion of history are not where Westhelle chooses to dwell because his eschatological endeavour above all searches for space. Theological thinking, Westhelle states, is so dependent on temporality, on the notion of history, that it lags behind other fields with regard to addressing geography and the importance of spatial issues.[4] When other fields turned geographical in the twentieth century, theology remained influenced by what Westhelle calls "one of the most militant voices against spatial thinking in theology", namely Paul Tillich.[5]

As we noted in Chapter 1, Tillich is not quite the abstract ontotheologian he is often made out to be—and many of Westhelle's examples from the history of theology could be similarly critically debated.[6] Yet Westhelle's general point about the Christian focus on history making "the rest of the world" come last—coming in from the lateral fringe or simply not finding a natural or rightful entry into theology in general—is compelling. Academic theology, it seems, needs to become explicitly postcolonial or else it will remain safely ensconced within the Western canon, writing and rewriting its history in a way that continues to exclude or marginalise most of the world.

A self-critical reflection serves to illustrate how apposite is this simple point. The historian Michel Foucault famously rewrote the Western histories of sexuality, sanity and punishment to show the limits of the habitually told histories in order to make visible who and what way of thinking did not fit in, as well as to indicate these histories' contingency. My previous book followed Foucault's art analyses through the course of his philosophical development and through the Western history of art. The two stories—that of Foucault's thinking and that of art—were told together with a third story that I added by reading between the lines of Foucault's texts: the story of Christianity moving from representation to performativity and materiality. But what if Foucault had written an essay on, say, the Peruvian indigenist artist José Sabogal (1888–1956) in between his essay on Velázquez and his lectures on Manet.[7] Where would I have discussed this imagined Sabogal essay? Where would the Peruvian artist fit into the three histories told in my book: Foucault's philosophical development, the history of painting, the (unorthodox) history of theology? In a separate chapter at the back? A history of the world is hard to keep together, as Kärkkinen's book on the holy spirit so well illustrates, which is why history tends to leave certain spaces blank. This strongly suggests that Westhelle is on to something, so let us hear what he has to say.

A theology of place

Westhelle tells this story in *Eschatology and Space* (2012): in the state of Paraná in southwest Brazil there was a camp for landless peasants. Around thirty families lived under the burning sun in tents made of black plastic. The place was a strip of land no more than twenty yards wide with the highway linking Brazil to Paraguay on the one side and the fence of a mega-farm on the other. After finishing his PhD in the 1970s, Westhelle worked as a minister in the area and one Sunday he and a Capuchin brother conducted a service in the camp. They read Psalm 24: "The earth is the Lord's and all that is in it, the world and those who live in it". One of the landless peasants, who had lost his family plot of land due to agrarian policies adopted by the military regime in the 1970s, raised his voice loud and clear: "If the earth is the Lord's how come that I only see this fence?" Westhelle was not only lost for words, he was lost for theology. Only studies in church architecture could be of some support in that situation, he recalls.[8] Theology failed him as a guide to framing *spatial* experiences.

He describes other similar situations all calling for a language, a thinking that would include spatial marginality, displacement and liminality as *theological* categories. Not as categories placed—or hidden—under ethics or morality, not theories of us helping those outside our history, at the fringes of our time, but actual theological categories for believers living at the margins: a proper theology of space, and a proper *eschatology* of space in particular. Westhelle thus rethinks the doctrine of the "last things", suggesting that we view eschatology as precisely the "things" that lie at the outskirts of the same, at the margins of the already familiar—as we traverse passageways, arcades, lobbies, roadways—yet especially experienced by those who have truly felt the materiality of the periphery. "Eschatology", he proposes, "is a discourse on liminality, marginality, on that which is in ontological, ethical, and also epistemological sense different".[9] For a spatial eschatology, last things are last not in time but in space. A spatial eschatology is about the experience of being in the margins, of being different, unorthodox, not according to plan, odd in relation to custom and tradition. In other words, for Westhelle the marginalised spaces, places on the edge, finally turn into the last things in spatial rather than temporal terms—turn into an actual eschatology.

This part of his reasoning is troublesome to me, however, since it makes the postcolonial voices stand forth as the eschatological choir singing from afar; the distant otherness that challenges *our* notions of time and space. They, the beggars, the others, their differences, teach *us* about eschatology. While I agree with Westhelle's general point concerning theological monovision when it comes to time and space, and I approve of his reminder of temporality as yet another expression of Western Christian oppression, a monovision of spatiality risks ending up in a similar place. Taking Westhelle's point into consideration, then, let us rethink the two in relation to each other and in relation to theological materiality—not to substitute time for space but to rethink both in order to open another space for thought. To do so we return, via Foucault, to the Russian Orthodox iconography and the liturgy discussed in Chapter 1. By way of Deleuze and our Russian constructors, we shall twist and bend the iconographic and liturgical timelessness of God until it includes a messiness of time and place—a messiness that concurs with current experiences of existence as threatened and out of hand, yet one that leaves open the possibility to act.

Radical liturgical theology

In the short but influential essay "Of Other Spaces: Utopias and Heterotopias" (1967), Michel Foucault describes "our era" as one of spatiality, whereas the nineteenth century is designated the era of temporality: "The great obsession of the nineteenth century was, as we know, history", he states before suggesting: "The present epoch will perhaps be above all the epoch of space".[10] There is much to say about Foucault's typically dramaturgical use of history; opposing one era to another, looking behind and ahead rather than sideways (in the ways we have just discussed). Still, his description of the late 1960s that follows is strikingly parallel to the current Western situation, with its merging of Internet connectivity and climate-change impacts affecting our notions of time and space. Foucault writes: "We are at a moment, I believe, when our experience of the world is less that of a long life developing through time than that of a network that connects points and intersects with its own skein". He describes how he is living in an "epoch of simultaneity: we are in the epoch of juxtaposition, the epoch of the near and far, of the side-by-side, of the dispersed".[11] Things appear juxtaposed, next to each other rather than stretched out in time.

The notion of space being stretched out in time is how Hegel argued that time and space were inevitably interconnected in his *Philosophy of Mind* in the 1820s: "The truth of space is time, so that space becomes time; our transition to time is not subjective, space itself makes the transition", Hegel wrote.[12] For Foucault, by 1967, things have changed and it is now the other way around. Time is stretched out in space. Time appears to us as space, as events on a surface—a point even more pertinent in the Internet era when time is presented as space; events of now and then, near and far, are juxtaposed and levelled out on a flat surface. Foucault's description of the epoch of space does in fact resemble the appearance of time and space in Russian iconography and Orthodox liturgy, which we encountered through Clemena Antonova in Chapter 1. Let us recapture the reasoning now that, unexpectedly, the timelessness of God portrayed in Orthodox services and icon art appear to coincide with the Foucauldian surface of appearances as a theological mystery of things. A slight reconstruction is all it takes to bring these together.

Antonova underlines the structural analogy between the artistic principle of the "supplementary planes" of the icon and the theological dogma of God's timelessness. In what appears as a distorted perspective, she argues, the icon depicts the world from the viewpoint of a timeless God. The many angles and planes depicted on the icon surface indicate a divine existence beyond time and space, an existence that consequently has no point of view but perceives all aspects of an object at once.[13] Heffermehl underlined this further by stating it is not about perspective at all but about presence, about viewing from within the material. Space is not stretched out in time but simultaneous, side by side. Time is laid out in space, on a flat surface. The icon painting technique thus indicates that beyond time there is no division between the future, the present and the past.

Though such a unity of diversity may appear almost unimaginable, thinkers like Pseudo-Dionysius the Areopagite do not easily give up the task of trying. Long before the Kantian limitations of human perception and the Hegelian assumptions of space-time, they wind, twist and bend language and thought to reach beyond. Pseudo-Dionusius argues, just as we cannot understand tangible things through abstraction, nor formless things through images, "the boundless Super-Essence surpasses Essence, the Super-Intellectual Unity surpasses Intelligences, the One which is beyond thought surpasses the apprehension of thought, and the Good which is beyond utterance surpasses the reach of words". To Pseudo-Dionusius, this limitless "Super-essence" is a unity: it is the One and is even "the unifying Source of all unity". It is "a Mind beyond the reach of mind" and "a Word beyond utterance, eluding Discourse, Intuition, Name, and every kind of being".[14] To him, in other words, it is all finally about the oneness of God—but just what does oneness mean at this stage of reasoning?

Antonova sees this radically transcendent notion, the oneness of God, reflected also in the Orthodox liturgy and its inconsistent use of present and future tenses.[15] She holds that liturgical time, understood through the notion of a timeless eternity—taking this divine existence as the presupposition for time—changes the understanding of temporality in Christian events. In Orthodox liturgical time, she argues, Christ's death and resurrection is not a once-and-for-all event seceding the before from the after, but an all-at-once phenomenon in a world grounded on timelessness. Linear time is changed to a mystical cyclical eternity in the present; or, as Evangolos Theodoron describes the experience of time in worship: Time ceases to exist in the form of past, present and future, and is changed into a mystical experience in which, while eternity is lived in the present, things of the past and of the future and even eschatological things—that is, prehistory and the main stages of the redemptive work of Christ, as well as the salutary gifts extending to the last days which followed from him—are condensed and experienced mystically as something living and present before our eyes.[16] In other words, the iconographic as well as the Orthodox liturgical practice eventuates in a diversity of time and perspectives in the present. Christianity becomes a multiplicity of events in the present, an assemblage of temporalities and a multiplicity of perspectives in space, an assemblage of angles—juxtaposed, side by side, a simultaneity of the near and far, a gathering of the dispersed. Time is crystallised, casting light in many directions at once, backwards and forwards. The logic of cause and effect is warped, the liturgical reality collapses the distinction between the actual and the virtual; real-time becomes a fiction, liturgical fiction becomes real-time. The virtually present is the actually present, the actually present is a delusion, or a virtuality. The past is what remains, the present is what passes and the two taken together with the eschatology that happens—the pastfuture/pastpresence/futurepresence—is what returns in the repetitive recurrent liturgical appearance as a constant construction of time and space.

Timemessiness and spacemessiness

In other words, we are following Pseudo-Dionysius closely in the sense that we are doing what he does; winding, twisting and bending words and thoughts. We bring the Orthodox timelessness into a Deleuzian timemessiness, without in fact doing much at all. In his two-volume work on cinema, Deleuze introduces the notion of *time crystals*, by way of Henri Bergson. Cinema has the ability to construct time crystals by linking unrelated fragments, thus rendering invisible forces visible in a course of events.[17] Or, rather, the earliest movie makers were committed to motion, to movement, to the possibility of the movement-image depicting the linearity of time as perceived by way of the main character—the subject's journey through time as a road laid out on the time-space of the screen surface. After the Second World War, Deleuze observes, something happened: cinema realised its ability to construct time-images. Dream-visions, memories and still-life scenes could be intermingled with the plot as plot, changing the very idea of the linearity of events. The virtual, as the set of potentials inherent in a pluriform past, could be present through actual events or fantasies, or simply through images of objects or landscapes, things or places. The time-images expressed crystals of time, the virtual could be expressed as a present past, carrying the potential of multiple futures, or pointing to an actualisation not taken, thus the time crystal would keep the virtual levelled with the actual.[18] Time, in other words, would appear as space, laid out on a surface of appearances: events juxtaposed on the mystery of things.

Deleuze exemplifies with Orson Welles' *Citizen Kane* (1941)—the movie making visible the vain hunt for the truth about Kane, the powerful media tycoon and wealthy entrepreneur. Who was he? What was the secret behind "Rosebud", his famous last word? The layers of stories, hopes, battles, the assemblage of subjective viewpoints, the many memories of others, of things he owned, his childhood sled—will they point towards the unity, the oneness, the *one* he was? Can he be glued back together to recreate the original unity? Is there a way to make a unity out of the heterogeneous bits? No, Deleuze concludes, there is no truth to Kane's life beyond what the witnesses have seen.[19]

Is there a truth to the life of Jesus apart from the assemblage of witnesses, apart from the memories, the dreams and desires connected with his name, the actualities and virtualities of his crystallised presence? Is the Christ-figure not, in that sense, truly a machine, even a cyborg? Is there a unity of God, is God a unity? Orthodox liturgy and iconography explicitly point to the divine One—to the unity that grounds the multiplicity of present times and perspectives—yet the one it performs is nothing like the ones we know. It performs, even materialises, a multiple time and a pluriform space. Or even, if we keep the notion of the one origin but twist it slightly, does not the liturgical and iconographic performance indicate that the ground of what we perceive as time and space is a lot messier than the categories themselves as they normally appear to us? Antonova makes clear that when the God perspective is brought into our time-space through liturgy and iconography, our world gets messed up: the perspective is necessarily plural, time is unavoidably condensed into a multiplicity of events in which linearity collapses. Hence, God beyond time, the cause of time and space, appears to have less symmetry than God's effects.[20] For the incarnated God, the haptic God, vision is all about viewing from within, at least in such a God-construction—a fabricated convergence of separate parts, working together but not unitary, à la Deleuze and Guattari.[21]

Such timemessiness eventuates in a spacemessiness as well. In *Religion, Space and the Environment* (2017), Sigurd Bergmann notes how the urban environment is dependent on amnesia, a spatial amnesia that has embraced change and constant re-presentation of the dynamics of the present. Still, a city has to treat its past somehow, and how it does so in the present, he reasons, is crucial for how it imagines the future.[21] The past is always there in the present, yet how a city is planned affects how we view this presence. Bergmann exemplifies this with cemeteries: Where are they placed—in the city centre or in the outskirts? Where is the place of the dead, of death? Where is my place for encounters with the passing of time, with the past-present? Bergmann even argues that a city that has evacuated the dead as far out to the periphery as possible is not to be trusted, and he quotes Dieter Hoffmann-Axthelm: "Obviously, in such a city nothing is arranged to abide and stay, why would I want to stay there?"[22]

Timemessiness eventuates in a spacemessiness when the iconograpic technique is brought together with the liturgical heterodoxy of time. Not only are the recto and the verso of a building both seen at once, but the past is placed next to the present. But not as an Eden lost or an End to come; rather, the many pasts and the many futures become a prism that makes out the present. The many pasts of a place, the lives that used to live there, the organisms that thrived, the critters, the grass, the trees. The simplified notion of past, present and future renders forgetfulness too easy—which in turn distances me from the many deaths, even extinctions, of which my life is part simply by being located.

The Christianity machine

Initially I stated that—to my own surprise—I have come to like Kärkkäinen's *Holy Spirit and Salvation* and teaching a rather traditional course on the holy spirit. The reason for this is that viewing Christianity through the variegated expressions of the Spirit—the many and often opposing pneumatologies through history and throughout the world, brought together during an intense winter month—does something. It makes Christianity stand forth as a multiplicity, as a machine forming a whole out of heterogenous bits. The Christianity machine, doing things all over the world, through time, different things called *Christian*.

No matter how far back in history you go, there is still no unity.[23] At times, the spirit is a phenomenon of nature, a wind; at times it is the opposite of nature, abstraction as such; or it is what preserves the order, the liturgy, the apostolic succession, the church institution, what unites the group; or it is what makes the individual stand up against it, what makes the minority group break with the majority tradition, what upsets, the unruly, the storm that makes one speak in tongues, that hands the truth of God to one who has never read a word; or spirit is that which makes you able to read and properly understand the word of God, the gentle breeze, what enlightens reason, the clear-thinking human ratio, even enables critical thought; it is what makes you certain, or what ensures you never know for sure; is that which transgresses the human mind, transcends human reality; or that which renders holy a particular human reality. In other words, there is no conformity whatsoever concerning what goes by the name of the holy spirit. To me, the workings of the spirit thus mirror the workings of the Christianity machine. A machine doing things called Christian simply because they relate to things that have been called Christian—such as certain actions, liturgies, books, houses, ideas, dreams, memories, hopes and such.

Perhaps Kärkkäinen would not appreciate what his book has come to mean to me, or maybe he would. His book tells me that Christianity is infinite because theology construction is infinite. The infinity of the spirit is right there on the book's pages—it is this-worldly yet enigmatic and *unstoppable*. It is in part beyond our control but in part a force serving our desire for change. Humbling yet empowering. Christianity as machine. In my view, that effect would only have been enhanced had the theologies all been introduced as an enigmatic web. African, North and South American, European, Asian, modern, medieval, now-then, here-there, side by side, juxtaposed. The placement of "the others" at the back lessens the mystery— a mystery of which I am a very small part. We are all laid out on a surface of times and places, next to each other; in each space, each particular place on this plane you may act, you may ask with Popova: "And Now? What next? This is the eternal question".[24]

Always onwards, always more, the question of the future, the next step—that is the principle of the artist's whole life, Popova writes; that is the principle of the artist's whole work.[25] She describes the history of art as an ongoing revolution, with the art of Christianity just as revolutionary with respect to the art it replaced as was the art of the middle ages, of the Renaissance, of the Baroque, the academicism, as is her and her contemporaries' reaction to the naturalism before them. Yet for her it is not only about a constant revolution through history, but also about the artist paving the way, "always with the revolutionary banner in the front rows of human assault".[26] Artists, she writes, "break through to new levels so that mankind can follow, at first rejecting, of course, but then accepting (after all, you have to go somewhere, and they cannot find the way themselves)".[27]

And there it is. There is the seed of totalitarianism right in the middle of the nuanced, complex, constructivist, nonrepresentational thinking of this egalitarian group of artists.[28] Bergmann's notion of amnesia and Westhelle's idea of history as grounding the dominance of *us* over *them* both prove accurate. *We* the artists now versus *them*, the people, or *them*, those of the past. Either way, the others "cannot find the way themselves". Popova finally reminds us of where we should not go, because suddenly we are not all laid out on a surface. Some are marching ahead, leaving others behind, on the sides, at the margin, in the past.

So, how might we ask Popova's question? In what sense would her question be relevant precisely as the eternal question—"And Now? What next?" How can it be asked in the situation we are in? Well, not as finally stating the way forwards in time and space but as a question posed to ourselves, to our place, and asked in humility towards the other critters and organisms, to matter and to the other places and times. The things present are always the last, we are all laid out on a surface. Now is the eschatology, now is the redemption, now is the death, now is the resurrection, now is the restoration, now is the reconstruction, now is the creation, now is the disaster, now is the recovery, right next to the impossible, always present. This is the now-time, *Jetztzeit*, to speak with Benjamin.

For Benjamin, history is not placed in a homogenous and empty structure called time, as Westhelle similarly notes, but time is always now-time, always filled to the brim, and every now has a gateway through which the Messiah may enter. This perspective is picked up also by the web of thinkers in contemporary theology, such as Swedish theologian Jayne Svenungsson and Catherine Keller.[29] Searching for a notion of time able to carry the time limits of climate change, Keller rereads Paul, "The appointed time is short" (1 Cor. 7:29), only to discover a new understanding of the verse. "Short", *sunestalemnos*, she notes, is more like "contracted", or "gathered together". The time that remains is contracted. It is a now-time in which all comes together and in which all come together.[30] In the everyday that evades us, the cutlery, the laundry, the dishes, the kisses, the quarrels, the bites, the stings, the mystery of desire, the mystery of things, the everyday dreamworld paralyses, inactivates—yet sparks and births change.[31] Next to us, now, is the construction—critters and thingies constructing the new, as they always do.

The cyborg has no origin, Haraway stated, and we have modelled our second-theology constructor on her cyborg. Second theology is about handling the relation between us and the Christian truths, I have suggested; it is to add rather than take away, to suggest rather than state, to construct rather than restore. A second theology is never about the origin as singular or final, which is why a second eschatology, similarly, is an eschatology without a fixed origin. We are always limited to the place where we are, to our everyday. And if there is no origin and no telos then what currently appears has no definitive other (i.e., nothing to define itself against) nor an original (i.e., nothing to mirror, to resemble) which means, in turn, that there is no limit to what the place can be, to what the everyday can be. The now-here, the fact that we always need a place to dwell—that reality in that sense is finite, is limited—makes life infinite, renders the possibilities of expression without end. And without a goal, for good and bad. If cyborgs inhabit the everyday—creatures with no definitive beginning or end—then theology construction is always also eschatological. Every now is an end and a beginning. Eschatology is always right next to us, the thingies next to us. Reality evades us, matter is enigmatic, so we need to take off our shoes when walking next to other critters, organisms, minerals, trees and melting ice. We should always be barefoot, but not inactive, because we are here now, like the other thingies. A Haraway quote, given a twist, sums it all up: No one lives everywhere (which is why God is such a messy no one) but everyone lives somewhere.[32]

Notes

1 Catherine Keller, *Political Theology of the Earth: Our Planetary Emergency and the Struggle for a New Public* (New York: Columbia University Press, 2018), 1.

2 George E. Tinker, *Spirit and Resistance: Political Theology and American Indian Liberation* (Augsburg: Fortress, 2004), 106.

3 Vitor Westhelle, *Eschatology and Space: The Lost Dimension in Theology Past and Present* (New York: Palgrave MacMillan, 2012), Kindle edition, 1569/4495.

4 Westhelle, *Eschatology and Space*, loc. 119/4495.

5 Westhelle, *Eschatology and Space*, loc. 144/4495.

6 Panu Pihkala, who discusses Tillich's contributions to ecotheological thought, notes that "Westhelle does not cite those writings of Tillich that demonstrate a material-oriented theology". Pihkala, *Early Ecotheology and Joseph Sittler*, 177. See also Swedish theologian Jayne Svenungsson's reinterpretation of Joachim of Fiore in Jayne Svenungsson, *Divining History: Prophetism, Messianism, and the Development of the Spirit*, trans. Stephen Donovan (Oxford: Berghahn, 2016).

7 Sigurd Bergmann discusses indigenist Peruvian art from an ethical, theological as well as aesthetical perspective as part of a larger argument in *I begynnelsen är bilden: En befriande bild-konst-kultur-teologi* (Uppsala: Proprius, 2003), 178.

8 Westhelle, *Eschatology and Space*, loc. 126/4495.

9 Westhelle, *Eschatology and Space*, loc. 1495/4495.

10 Michel Foucault, "Of Other Spaces: Utopias and Heterotopias", in *The Visual Culture Reader*, 2nd ed., ed. Nicholas Mirzoeff (London: Routledge, 2002), 229–235, 229.

11 Foucault, "Of Other Spaces: Utopias and Heterotopias", 229.

12 Cited and discussed by Bart Zantvoort in the excellent "Space-Time Dialectics: Acceleration and the Politics of Space", *Azimuth* 10 (2018), 105–118.

13 Clemena Antonova, "On the Problem of 'Reverse Perspective': Definitions East and West", *Leonardo* 43, no. 5 (2010): 464–469, 467.

14 From Pseudo-Dionusius the Areopagite, "*The Divine Names 1.1* (Rolt translation, 51–53)" in *Holy Spirit and Salvation: The Sources of Christian Theology*, ed. Veli-Matti Kärkkäinen (Louisville: Westminster John Knox, 2010), 104–105.

15 Antonova, *Space, Time, and Presence in the Icon*, 132.

16 Antonova, *Space, Time, and Presence in the Icon*, 135.

17 Gilles Deleuze, *Cinema II*, trans. Hugh Tomlison and Robert Galeta (Minneapolis: University of Minnesota Press, 1989), 82. See also Philip Goodchild, *Deleuze and Guattari: An Introduction to the Politics of Desire* (London: Sage, 1996), 190.

18 See also Jon Bialecki and James S. Bielo, "The Ancient-Future Time-Crystal: On the Temporality of Emerging Christianity", unpublished paper, cited with permission.

19 Deleuze, *Cinema II*, 105.

20 "What matters is the possibility of the cause having less symmetry than the effect". Gilles Deleuze, *Difference and Repetition*, trans. Paul Patton (New York: Continuum, 2004), 22.

21 Bergmann, *Religion, Space and the Environment*, 87.

22 Bergmann, *Religion, Space and the Environment*, 93.

23 For the many origins of Christianity, see also Samuel Rubenson, "Textual Fluidity in Early Monasticism: Sayings, Sermons, and Stories", in *Snapshots of Evolving Traditions: Jewish and Christian Manuscript Culture, Textual Fluidity, and New Philology*, eds. Liv Ingeborg Lied and Hugo Lundhaug (Boston: de Gruyter, 2017), 178–200.

24 Popova, "From Materials for a Speech on Style", in *Liubov Popova*, eds. Dimitri V. Sarabianov and Natalia L. Adaskina, trans. Marian Schwartz (New York: Harry N. Abrams, 1990), 356.

25 Ibid.

26 Ibid.

27 Ibid.

28 While theorists such as Christina Kiaer and Christina Lodder underline the fundamental differences between the constructivist movement and the political ideology of the Soviet regime, Russian-German thinker and writer Boris Groys underlines, instead, the similarities. The very idea of art as practice, as a constructivism of lived reality involves an aspiration for power, he argues. The rigid control of the masses that developed in the years after the revolution, he argues, was not at odds with but in fact fully congruent with the very nuclear of the artistic avantgarde. See Boris Groys, *Avantgardet och samlingens logik* (Nørhaven: Site Editions/Propexus, 2012), 31.

29 Jayne Svenungsson, "Tradition and Transformation: Towards a Messianic Critique of Religion", in *Phenomenology and Religion: New Frontiers*, eds. Jonna Bornemark and Hans Ruin (Huddinge: Södertörn University, 2010), 205–222; Keller, *Political Theology of the Earth*, 60–61.

30 Keller, *Political Theology of the Earth*, 3.

31 This footnote is all that is left of my starting point for writing on the everyday, namely reading Henri Lefebvre on the "ill-defined zone of the everyday". Henri Lefebvre, "Myths in Everyday Life", in *Henri Lefebvre: Key Writings*, eds. Stuart Elden, Elizabeth Lebas, and Eleonore Kofman (London: Bloomsbury, 2003), 112–119, 112.

32 Haraway, *Staying with the Trouble*, 31.

Conclusion
Second theology: a manifesto

1. For second theology, construction is the only given

Not truth, but the relation between humanity and Christian truths—that is what second-theology constructors deal with, and that is enough. Because when construction is understood as a given, almost nothing else is. And others can do other things.

2. Second theology is always political

This simply follows from 1.

3. Construction works with an infinity of screws, planks, circuit boards, inherited ideas and hands

Construction without a definitive *other* is limitless—for good or bad. If someone asserts it is not the case, show them it is. The infinity of construction can lead to respect and humility, even to love. And also to action and activism, since we are constructors. Not creators, but mechanics, like the rest.

4. Christ is a machine

The Christ machine is a perpetual machine, dying and resurrecting in times and places, pasts and presents, a repetition of difference. An ongoing construction made out of heterogenous bits. Not the normative face but screws and gears of multiplicity, even in faces. Which is why it is all about tenderness towards the constructions we have/are, about encounters, and a sense of possibility.

5. Trees make us take off our shoes, as do compasses, and critters, cyborgs, faces and stuff

The mystery is the infinity of construction present in every spot on the reality plane, and it is as holy as it gets.

6. Eschatology is about the thingies next to us, because they are always the last

Eschatology is now, over there and right here, a dimension of the present. Sadly, no final salvation is to be expected, yet infinite possibilities are right here, even if inactive.

7. God is a thingie

God is a word, an idea, a machine, a thing, and those are finite, as we are.

8. Finitude enables construction

Construction is infinite only if things have no definitive other, whether out there, back then or way ahead—that is, if they are finite.

8.5. Placards whither

Bibliography

Natalia Adaskina, "Part Two: Theory, Teaching, and Design", in Dimitri V. Sarabianov and Natalia L. Adaskina, eds., *Liubov Popova*, trans. Marian Schwartz (New York: Harry N. Abrams, 1990), 190–307.

Giorgio Agamben, *The Mystery of Evil: Benedict and the End of Days*, trans. Adam Kotsko (Stanford: Stanford University Press, 2017).

Clemena Antonova, "On the Problem of 'Reverse Perspective': Definitions East and West", in *Leonardo* 43, no. 5 (2010): 464–469.

Clemena Antonova, *Space, Time, and Presence in the Icon: Seeing the World with the Eyes of God* (London: Routledge, 2009).

Christopher Baugh, *Theatre, Performance and Technology: The Development and Transformation of Scenography* (Basingstoke: Palgrave Macmillan, 2013).

Walter Benjamin, "The Work of Art in the Age of Mechanical Reproduction", in Hannah Arendt, ed., *Illuminations*, trans. Harry Zohn (New York: Schocken, 1969), 217–252.

Walter Benjamin, "The Work of Art in the Age of Its Technological Reproducibility: Second Version", in Michael W. Jennings, Bridgid Doherty, and Thomas Y. Levin, eds., *The Work of Art in the Age of Its Technological Reproducibility and Other Writings on Media*, trans. Edmund Jephcott, Rodney Livingstone, Howard Eiland, and others (Cambridge: Harvard University Press, 2008), 19–55.

Sigurd Bergmann, *In the Beginning is the Icon: A Liberative Theology of Images, Visual Arts and Culture* (London: Routledge, 2016).

Sigurd Bergmann, *Religion, Space and the Environment* (New York: Routledge, 2017).

Christine Blaettler, "Phantasmagoria: A Profane Phenomenon as a Critical Alternative to the Fetish", in *Image and Narrative* 13, no. 1 (2012): 32–47.

Ward Blanton, Clayton Crockett, Jeffrey W. Robbins, and Noëlle Vahanian, eds., *An Insurrectionist Manifesto: Four New Gospels for a Radical Politics* (New York: Columbia University Press, 2016).

Svetlana Boym, "From the Russian Soul to Post-Communist Nostalgia", in *Representations* 49 (1995): 133–166.

Edward Braun, *Meyerhold: A Revolution in Theatre* (Wallington: Methuen Drama, 1998).

Virginia Burrus, *Ancient Christian Ecopoetics: Cosmologies, Saints, Things* (Philadelphia: University of Pennsylvania Press, 2019).

94 *Bibliography*

Petra Carlsson, "Foucault, Velazquez and the Place of Theology", in *Studia Theologica: Nordic Journal of Theology* 69, no. 2 (2015): 126–149.

John Powell Clayton, *The Concept of Correlation: Paul Tillich and the Possibility of a Mediating Theology* (New York: de Gruyter, 1980).

James H. Cone, *The Cross and the Lynching Tree* (New York: Orbis, 2013).

Catherine de Zegher, "A Century Under the Sign of Line: Drawing and Its Extensions (1910–2010)", in Cornelia H. Butler and Catherine de Zegher, eds., *On Line: Drawing Through the Twentieth Century* (New York: Museum of Modern Art, 2010), 21–124.

Gilles Deleuze, *Cinema II*, trans. Hugh Tomlison and Robert Galeta (Minneapolis: University of Minnesota Press, 1989).

Gilles Deleuze, *Difference and Repetition*, trans. Paul Patton (New York: Continuum, 2004).

Gilles Deleuze and Felix Guattari, *A Thousand Plateaus: Capitalism and Schizophrenia*, trans. Brian Massumi (London: Athlone, 1999).

Celia Deane Drummond, *Eco-Theology* (Winona: Saint Mary's Press, 2008).

Celia-Deane Drummond, Sigurd Bergmann, and Bronislaw Szerszynski, *Technofutures, Nature and the Sacred* (Farnham: Ashgate, 2015).

Briony Fer, "What's in a Line? Gender and Modernity", in *The Oxford Journal of Modern Art* 13, no. 1 (1990): 77–88.

Pavel Florensky, "Reverse Perspective", in Nicoletta Misher, ed., *Beyond Vision: Essays on the Perception of Art*, trans. Wendy Salmond (London: Reaktion, 2002), 197–272.

Michel Foucault, "Of Other Spaces: Utopias and Heterotopias", in Nicholas Mirzoeff, ed., *The Visual Culture Reader*, 2nd ed. (London: Routledge, 2002), 229–235.

Pope Francis, *Laudato Si: On Care for Our Common Home* (Vatican City: Vatican Press, 2015).

M. I. Franklin, "Reading Walter Benjamin and Donna Haraway in the Age of Digital Reproduction", in *Information, Communication and Society* 5, no. 4 (2010): 591–624.

Laurel Fredrickson, "Vision and Material Practice: Vladimir Tatlin and the Design of Everyday Objects", in *Design Issues* 15, no. 1 (Spring 1999), 49–74.

Maria Gough, "Faktura: The Making of the Russian Avant-Garde", in *Res* 36 (Autumn 1999): 32–59.

Boris Groys, *Avantgardet och samlingens logik* (Nørhaven: Site Editions/Propexus, 2012).

Olav Hammer and Michael Rothstein, eds., *Handbook of the Theosophical Current* (Leiden: Brill, 2013).

Donna Haraway, "A Manifesto for Cyborgs: Science, Technology, and Socialist Feminism in the 1980s", in Linda J. Nicholson, ed., *Feminism/Postmodernism* (New York: Routledge, 1990), 191–233.

Donna Haraway, *The Companion Species Manifesto: Dogs, People, and Significant Others* (Chicago: University of Chicago Press, 2003).

Donna Haraway, in an interview by Nicholas Gane, "When We Have Never Been Human, What is to Be Done? Interview with Donna Haraway", in *Theory, Culture and Society* 23, no. 7–8 (2006): 135–158.

Donna Haraway, *When Species Meet* (Minneapolis: University of Minnesota Press, 2007).

Donna Haraway, *Staying with the Trouble: Making Kin in the Chthulucene* (Durham: Duke University Press, 2016).

Donna Haraway, *Making Kin not Population: Reconceiving Generations* (Chicago: Prickly Paradigm, 2018).

Louise Hardiman and Nicola Kozicharow, "Introduction", in Louise Hardiman and Nicola Kozicharow, eds., *Modernism and the Spiritual in Russian Art: New Perspectives*, (Cambridge: Open Books, 2017), 9–36.

Fabian Heffermehl, *Bildet sett fra innsiden: Ikonoklastiske og matematiske konsepter i Florenskijs omvendte perspektiv* (Uppsala: Uppsala University, 2015).

Hugo von Hofmannsthal, "The Letter of Lord Chandos", trans. Tania Stern and James Stern, in *Jubilat*, no. 11; http://www.jubilat.org/jubilat/archive/vol11/poem_10/.

Brad J. Kallenberg, *God and Gadgets: Following Jesus in a Technological Age* (Oregon: Cascade, 2011).

Catherine Keller, *Face of the Deep: A Theology of Becoming* (New York: Routledge, 2003).

Catherine Keller, *Political Theology of the Earth: Our Planetary Emergency and the Struggle for a New Public* (New York: Columbia University Press, 2018).

Christina Kiaer, *Imagine No Possessions: The Socialist Objects of Russian Constructivism* (Cambridge: MIT, 2005).

Christina Kiaer, "The Short Life of the Equal Woman: Remembering the Work of Russian Female Artists Under Stalin in the 1930s", in *TATE ETC* (20 October 2017), https://www.tate.org.uk/tate-etc/issue-15-spring-2009/short-life-equal-women, accessed 1 September 2018.

Leonard Lawlor, "Following the Rats: An Essay on the Concept of Becoming-Animal in Deleuze and Guattari", in *Sub-Stance* 37, no. 3(117) on "The Political Animal" (2008): 169–187.

Henri Lefebvre, "Myths in Everyday Life", in Stuart Elden, Elizabeth Lebas and Eleonore Kofman, eds., *Henri Lefebvre: Key Writings* (London: Bloomsbury, 2003), 112–119.

Robert Jay Lifton, *The Protean Self: Human Resilience in an Age of Fragmentation* (Chicago: University of Chicago Press, 1993).

Christina Lodder, "The Transition to Constructivism", in Paul Wood, ed., *The Great Utopia: The Russian and Soviet Avant-Garde, 1915–1932* (New York: Guggenheim Museum, 1994), 267–281.

Christina Lodder, "Liubov Popova: From Painting to Textile Design", in *Tate Papers*, no. 14 (Autumn 2010), https://www.tate.org.uk/research/publications/tate-papers /14/liubov-popova-from-painting-to-textile-design, accessed 20 October 2018.

Christina Lodder, "Conflicting Approaches to Creativity? Suprematism and Constructivism", in Christina Lodder, ed., *Celebrating Suprematism: New Approaches to Kazimir Malevich* (Leiden: Brill, 2019), 259–288.

Argyro Loukaki, *The Geographical Unconscious* (New York: Routledge, 2014).

Vladimir Markov, "The Principles of Creativity in the Plastic [Visual] Arts: *Faktura*", trans. Jeremy Howard, in Jeremy Howard, Irena Buzinska, and Z. S. Strother, eds., *Vladimir Markov and Russian Primitivism: A Charter for the Avant-Garde* (Farnham: Ashgate, 2015), 179–216.

Lissa McCullough, "D. G. Leahy", in Christopher D. Rodkey and Jordan E. Miller, eds., *Palgrave Handbook of Radical Theology* (New York: Palgrave Macmillan, 2019), 269–280.

Scott Midson, *Cyborg Theology: Humans, Technology and God* (London: I.B. Tauris, 2017).

Scott Midson, "Humus and Sky Gods: Partnership and Post/Humans in Genesis 2 and the Chthulucene", in *Sofia* 58 (2018): 689–698.

Jordan E. Miller, *Resisting Theology, Furious Hope: Secular Political Theology and Social Movements* (New York: Palgrave Macmillan, 2019).

Charles Mills, *The Racial Contract* (Ithaca: Cornell University Press, 1999).

John Milner, *Vladimir Tatlin and the Russian Avantgarde* (New Haven: Yale University Press, 1983).

Katharine Sarah Moody, *Radical Theology and Emerging Christianity: Deconstruction, Materialism and Religious Practices* (Dorchester: Ashgate, 2015).

Daniel Mourenza, "Dreams of a Better Nature: Walter Benjamin on the Creation of a Collective Techno-Body", in *Teknokultura: Revista de Cultura Digital y Movimientos Sociales* 10, no. 3 (2013): 693–718.

Robert Nelson, *The Spirit of Secular Art: A History of the Sacramental Roots of Contemporary Artistic Values* (Clayton: Monash University Epress, 2007).

Andreas Nordlander, "Green Purpose, Teleology, Ecological Ethics, and the Recovery of Contemplation", *Studies in Christian Ethics*, first published online: March 4, 2020, https://doi.org/10.1177%2F0953946820910672.

Michael Northcott, *The Environment and Christian Ethics* (Cambridge: Cambridge University Press, 1996).

Michael Northcott, "Lynn White Jr. Right and Wrong: The Anti-Ecological Character of Latin Christianity, and the Pro-Ecological Turn of Protestantism", in T. le Vasseur and A. Peterson, eds., *Religion and Ecological Crisis: The "Lynn White Thesis" at 50* (New York: Routledge, 2016), 61–74.

John Paul II, *Common Declaration of Environmental Ethics: Common Declaration of John Paul II and the Ecumenical Patriarch His Holiness Bartholomew I* (Rome: Libreria Editrice Vaticana, 2002).

Panu Pihkala, *Early Ecotheology and Jospeh Sittler* (Zurich: LIT, 2017).

Sarah K. Pinnock, ed., *The Theology of Dorothee Sölle* (Harrisburg: Trinity Press International, 2003).

Liubov Popova, "The Essence of the Disciplines", in Dimitri V. Sarabianov and Natalia L. Adaskina, eds., *Liubov Popova*, trans. Marian Schwartz (New York: Harry N. Abrams, 1990), 369–371.

Liubov Popova, "For the Museum of Artistic Culture", in Dimitri V. Sarabianov and Natalia L. Adaskina, eds., *Liubov Popova*, trans. Marian Schwartz (New York: Harry N. Abrams, 1990), 359.

Liubov Popova, "On a Precise Criterion, on Ballet Steps, on Deck Equipment for Warships, on Picasso's Latest Portraits, and on the Observation Tower at the Military Camouflage School at Kuntsevo (a Few Thoughts that Came to Mind During the Vocal and Ballet Numbers at the Krivoi Dzhimmi Summer Theater in Moscow in the Summer of 1922)", in Dimitri V. Sarabianov and Natalia L. Adaskina, eds., *Liubov Popova*, trans. Marian Schwartz (New York: Harry N. Abrams, 1990), 380–381.

Liubov Popova, "The Question of the New Methodology of Instruction (First Discipline of the Basic Department of the Vkhutemas Painting Faculty)", in Dimitri V. Sarabianov and Natalia L. Adaskina, eds., *Liubov Popova*, trans. Marian Schwartz (New York: Harry N. Abrams, 1990), 375–377.

Liubov Popova, "Statement from the Catalog for the 'Tenth State Exhibition: Nonobjective Art and Suprematism'", in Dimitri V. Sarabianov and Natalia L. Adaskina, eds., *Liubov Popova*, trans. Marian Schwartz (New York: Harry N. Abrams, 1990), 346–347.

Sofia Proofh, *Gläd er och jubla ständigt över det som jag skapar: En jämförande textanalys om djurrätt och miljöpåverkan ur ett teologiskt perspektiv*, kandidatuppsats, Stockholm School of Theology, 2018.

Pseudo-Dionusius the Areopagite, "*The Divine Names* 1.1 (Rolt translation, 51–53)", in Veli-Matti Kärkkäinen, ed., *Holy Spirit and Salvation: The Sources of Christian Theology* (Louisville: Westminster John Knox, 2010), 104–105.

Elena Rakitin, "How Meierkhol'd Never Worked with Tatlin, and What Happened as a Result", in Paul Wood, ed., *The Great Utopia: The Russian and Soviet Avantgarde 1915–1932* (New York: Guggenheim Museum, 1992), 649–664.

Russell Re Manning, *Theology at the End of Culture: Paul Tillich's Theology of Culture and Art* (Leuven: Peeters, 2005).

Russell Re Manning, "Tillich's Theology of Art", in Russell Re Manning, ed., *The Cambridge Companion to Paul Tillich* (Cambridge: Cambridge University Press, 2008), 152–172.

Russell Re Manning, ed., *Retrieving the Radical Tillich: His Legacy and Contemporary Importance* (New York: Palgrave Macmillan, 2015).

Jeffrey W. Robbins, "Changing Ontotheology: Paul Tillich, Catherine Malabou, and the Plastic God", in Russell Re Manning, ed., *Retrieving the Radical Tillich: His Legacy and Contemporary Importance* (New York: Palgrave Macmillan, 2015), 159–177.

Jeffrey W. Robbins, *Radical Theology: A Vision for Change* (Bloomington: Indiana University Press, 2016).

Terra Schwerin Rowe, *Toward a Better Worldliness: Ecology, Economy, and the Protestant Tradition* (Minneapolis: Fortress, 2017).

Samuel Rubenson, "Textual Fluidity in Early Monasticism: Sayings, Sermons, and Stories", in Liv Ingeborg Lied and Hugo Lundhaug, eds., *Snapshots of Evolving Traditions: Jewish and Christian Manuscript Culture, Textual Fluidity, and New Philology* (Boston: de Gruyter, 2017), 178–200.

Tom Sandqvist, *Det andra könet i öst: Om kvinnliga konstnärer i den central- och östeuropeiska modernismen* (Stockholm: Symposium, 2010).

Laurel C. Schneider, "The Courage to See and to Sin: Mary Daly's Elemental Transformation of Paul Tillich's Ontology", in Sarah Lucia Hoagland and Marilyn Frye, eds., *Feminist Interpretations of Mary Daly* (University Park: Pennsylvania State University Press, 2000), 55–75.

Laurel C. Schneider, *Beyond Monotheism: A Theology of Multiplicity* (New York: Routledge, 2008).

Dorothee Sölle, *On Earth as in Heaven: A Liberation Spirituality of Sharing* (Louisville: Westminster John Knox, 1993).

Andrew Spira, *The Avant-Garde Icon: Russian Avant-Garde Art and the Icon Painting Tradition* (Burlington: Lund Humphries, 2008).

98   Bibliography

Jayne Svenungsson, "Tradition and Transformation: Towards a Messianic Critique of Religion", in Jonna Bornemark and Hans Ruin, eds., *Phenomenology and Religion: New Frontiers* (Huddinge: Södertörn University, 2010), 205–222.

Jayne Svenungsson, *Divining History: Prophetism, Messianism, and the Development of the Spirit*, trans. Stephen Donovan (Oxford: Berghahn, 2016).

Jayne Svenungsson, "Interdependence and the Biblical Legacy of Anthropocentrism: On Human Destructiveness and Human Responsibility", in *Eco-Ethica* 7 (August 8, 2018): 35–47.

Bronislaw Szerszynsky, *Nature, Technology and the Sacred* (Oxford: Blackwell, 2005).

Joan E. Taylor, *What Did Jesus Look Like?* (London: Bloomsbury T & T Clark, 2018).

Mark C. Taylor, *Disfiguring: Art, Architecture, Religion* (Chicago: Chicago University Press, 1992).

John Thatamanil, "Tillich and the Postmodern", in Russell Re Manning, ed., *The Cambridge Companion to Paul Tillich* (Cambridge: Cambridge University Press, 2009), 288–302.

Paul Tillich, *Systematic Theology I* (Chicago: University of Chicago Press, 1951).

Paul Tillich, *Biblical Religion and the Search for Ultimate Reality*, 1st ed. (Chicago: University of Chicago Press, 1955).

Paul Tillich, "Lecture 2: Culture, Society, and Art", trans. Robert P. Scharlemann, in John Dillenberger and Jane Dillenberger, eds., *Paul Tillich on Art and Architecture* (New York: Crossroad, 1987), 21–31.

Paul Tillich, "The Problem of Theological Method (1947)", in John Clayton, ed., *Paul Tillich: Main Works 4, Writings in the Philosophy of Religion* (New York: de Gruyter, 1987), 301–312.

Paul Tillich, *The Religious Situation* (2003), file:///D:/rb/relsearchd.dll-action=show item&gotochapter=3&id=18.htm (2 of 7) [2/4/03 1:42:14 PM], accessed 1 June 2018.

George E. Tinker, *Spirit and Resistance: Political Theology and American Indian Liberation* (Augsburg: Fortress, 2004).

Mark I. Wallace, *When God Was a Bird: Christianity, Animism, and the Re-Enchantment of the World* (New York: Fordham University Press, 2019).

Vitor Westhelle, *Eschatology and Space: The Lost Dimension in Theology Past and Present* (New York: Palgrave MacMillan, 2012).

Lynn White Jr., "The Historical Roots of Our Ecologic Crisis", in *Science* 155, no. 3767 (10 March 1967): 1203–1207.

Espeth Whitney, "Lynn White Jr.'s 'The Historical Roots of Our Ecological Crisis' After 50 Years", in *History Compass* 13, no. 8 (2015): 396–410.

M. N. Yablonskaya, *Women Artists of Russia's New Age: 1900–1935* (London: Thames and Hudson, 1990).

Index

Note: Page numbers in italics indicate figures.

Printed in Great Britain
by Amazon

20128407R00071